"This book presents one of the first views from inside a new type of monastery in the church. Drawing on John Michael Talbot's twenty-five plus years in community, it breathes the air of honest-to-God daily experience of monastic life, and in a very complex type of community, comprising celibates, marrieds, singles, and children. The new monasticism, with its many ways of participating, provides access from wherever you are into an ancient contemplative path."

—*Abbot Jerome Kodell, OSB*
Subiaco Abbey, Arkansas

"John Michael Talbot is the real deal. Here is a guide to new monasticism that exudes wisdom and carefully considers the questions that have arisen through decades of practice. If you're serious about asking what monasticism means for the church today—about what it means for you—read this book."

—*Jonathan Wilson-Hartgrove*
Author of New Monasticism
Co-compiler of Common Prayer:
A Liturgy for Ordinary Radicals
Member of the Rutba House community in
Durham, North Carolina

The Universal Monk
The Way of the New Monastics

John Michael Talbot

LITURGICAL PRESS
Collegeville, Minnesota

www.litpress.org

| 1 | 2 | 3 | 4 | 5 | 6 | 7 | 8 | 9 |

Library of Congress Cataloging-in-Publication Data

Talbot, John Michael.
    The universal monk : the way of the new monastics / John Michael Talbot.
      p. cm.
    ISBN 978-0-8146-3341-0 — ISBN 978-0-8146-3951-1 (e-book)
    1. Christian life—Catholic authors.　2. Monastic and religious life—
Miscellanea.　3. Communities—Religious aspects—Catholic Church.
I. Title.
    BX2350.3.T35 2011
    271'.3—dc22
                                       2010052672

Contents

Introduction
The Universal Monk, the Way of the New Monastics

There is a new monasticism on the rise. It is monasticism for everyone, for all states of life, and for people of all faiths. It is for those who live in monasteries and for those who do not. It speaks to the monk within us all, the universal monk. But it also calls those who long to live in monasteries, and to those who already do. From it the Spirit is raising new monasteries up for our time.

Much like the early monks of Egypt this is a charismatic phenomenon of the Spirit. It is the result not merely of good ideas but of the Spirit stirring within people's hearts. The Spirit is calling us to something more than what is normally available in the parish church or the secular world. Like the first Christian monks of the desert, this stirring of the Spirit cannot be stopped or manipulated. It is a sovereign work of God in the hearts and souls of people. But it can, at least to some degree, be described.

The essential characteristic of these new monasteries is the contemplative life for all people from all states of life that overflows into action that changes the world for the better. These communities become workshops of prayer that is tested and tried in some form of community life. It is in solitude that we find deeper meditation and contemplative union with God. It is in community that the authenticity of that union is tested and tried. When the two come together, they are called "communion" or "common union." That form is based on ancient monastic patterns but is adapted to modern life.

There are several better-known published current streams in the new monasticism today. The first, and most widely known, is the new monasticism from the Baptist tradition (they actually coined the phrase) that emphasizes an evangelical, community-based social justice movement. This is reminiscent of the communities of the late 1960s that are not so much monastic as simply communal. The second is an interfaith integrated monasticism that values the theology of folks like Raimon Pannikar. This is also in the stream of Bede Griffiths's vision and dream. The "New Friars" are a social justice community based on Franciscan spirituality. Also, the Boiler Room evangelical and interdenominational communities of Europe, sometimes called the "Punk Monk" movement, used the Rule of St. Benedict when looking for an established rule for more intense community living. But there is much more.

I write this book at the invitation of Liturgical Press from the perspective of a founder of one of these many new monastic expressions within the Catholic Christian tradition. They are being raised up everywhere, from the ancient Christian countries of Europe to Hindu India to our own religiously pluralistic United States and Canada. Most communities include some integrated form of monastic community that serves as a base, as well as those who live in their own homes who associate with those monasteries in some meaningful way. Alternative forms of community life and powerful new ministries are spreading the word to all who will listen. It is a true phenomenon of the Spirit.

These monastic expressions can be traditional or new, or both. In the Catholic Church after Vatican II, many new forms of community have come and gone. A few have persevered. Some of these were overly experimental, but some were properly creative. The use of the Rule of St. Benedict has been inevitable by some, and most surprisingly by the new monasticism movement within the Anabaptist tradition. There are also new expressions in almost every major religious family in the church. With the recent conservative swing in the Catholic Church, communities that attempt to reestablish traditional patterns of consecrated life within the established spiritual families are numerous. There are also completely new communities that are both conservative and progressive. At the beginning of the appearance of these new communities, an integration of spiritualities and states of life and the empowerment of the laity was pretty normative. Today the more conservative communities are moving back into old models. Some of this is good, and some of it is a matter for concern. The church is watching all of this unfold with great interest in order to assist where she may to help facilitate this wind of the Spirit who is raising up these new monastic communities and associations.

I write from the perspective of my own experience in the community I helped found. After the ideal of simple gospel living, our community is based on the ideal of integration. We integrate states of life and spiritualities. We have celibates, singles who can marry, and families in one monastic community. We also have domestics (based on the word "domicile," or "home") who live around the country and the world in their own homes. We integrate solitude and community with hermits and community dwellers, a contemplative base and active ministry. We also integrate charismatic and contemplative, liturgical and spontaneous spiritualities. Some have said that we have integrated too much to keep a more narrow focus. We believe that these integrations are a sign and hope for the church in the future.

It has taken a few decades to see our community unfold, and it is still unfolding with its first generation of members. In this book I will discuss the vision of our community, how it fits in the church and the world, and where it may still develop.

To illustrate the new interest in integrated monastic communities, a story might be helpful. My wife and I were once asked to address a Benedictine congregation's general chapter about integrated monasticism as a possible way of revitalizing older communities that are closing due to low numbers. I gave a normal presentation of our integrated monastic life, and it met with a reserved, favorable response. I did not get the impression that these abbots were all that anxious to go out and try the integrated model!

I was then disheartened when the next speaker gave his presentation. He is an abbot from a community in Europe that had tried the integrated model and failed. At first I felt like my talk had been completely torpedoed. But as I listened further, I realized that he was actually affirming our new integrated monastic community.

Interestingly, it did not work in the older monastery because the lay community brought such life and did so much of the needed work that unforeseen rivalry between the older celibate community and the lay community inevitably arose. Though the abbot came from the lay community, one of his first actions as abbot was to formally separate the lay monastic community from the older celibate community and find them a new facility in which to live and from which to minister. They have prospered ever since. But that is not the point.

The abbot shared his belief that ultimately many of the older monasteries will inevitably pass away and that new monasteries will be birthed from the lay communities themselves. This filled me with affirmation and hope.

This is really our experience as well. We tried a new model with traditional Franciscans at a retreat center, but it didn't really work. Ultimately we had to move away and start fresh in order for the new model to work without hindrance.

As founder, I received three "words" that helped us with this process. The first said not to put "new wine into old wineskins." The second said to "die to Franciscanism." The third was to "build community by not building community." The community received these words enthusiastically, but living them out has been a process. The first two were pretty easy to understand but not easy to do. I have a great love of all things Franciscan, and finding a church home in pastoral practice, or in canon law, is far from easy to accomplish.

The third was most enigmatic, and we are still discovering its deeper meaning. We believe it means that it is more important to live and share the content of community life than to simply propagate its outer form. It is tempting to promote an organization but much harder to spiritually grow a living community.

But this is not the end of the story. After founding the monastery on ancient but new ideals, we have continued to develop. We were birthed from a few dreamers who came mainly from the Jesus Movement of the late 1960s and early 1970s and found greater ancient roots and gospel radicalism in monasticism and the Catholic faith. We also included those who were Catholic from birth. At the beginning, we were very orthodox in our Catholic faith but also very open ecumenically. Today we are still orthodox but are going deeper into the contemplative tradition that is appropriately open to interfaith dialogue and experience. While retaining our orthodox base, we have found these ecumenical and interfaith integrations most enriching.

We are also reaching out in ministry. As we travel around the world and share the gospel message, we are finding that there are thousands interested in living a monastic spirituality at home in the secular world with some form of loose-knit associational community. They are not called to join the monastic expression as such, but they are called to participate in some meaningful way.

We are seeing a renewed interest in our domestic expression. We are starting new groups that emphasize simple gospel living and meditation that lead to deeper understanding of Jesus, the church, and our place in the modern world. Some of these members join our community as domestics or monastics. Some do not. Either way is OK as long as we are bringing them closer to Jesus who renews their life through changed lifestyle and meditative prayer.

Almost eight hundred years ago St. Bonaventure wrote in his *Collations on the Six Days of Creation* of the "Contemplative Church of the Future" that would be poor like Jesus and a "Seraphic Order" of contemplatives that would include and transcend all orders and states of life (see col. 22). It would confirm and be rooted in the old, but progress in the Spirit into the new. I believe that this prophecy is no less true today than it was over seven hundred years ago. In fact, as it was being realized in the new religious orders of St. Bonaventure's time, so it is still being realized today.

This book will be an attempt to present some of the teachings on community and prayer that are being met with such great success by so many. I pray that you will join me as we go deeper into the subjects mentioned only briefly in this introduction.

Basics

A lmost every monastic rule begins with a statement of basic vision. For Christian monks, it is usually living the gospel in a more intense way. For Franciscans, it is "observing the gospel of our Lord Jesus Christ." For Benedictines, it is found in various statements in the Rule of St. Benedict like, "Prefer nothing whatever to Christ," or establishing a "school of the Lord's service." The prologue and first seven chapters of this rule form a spiritual core from which all the other sixty-five chapters flow.

The same is true of our new monastic community. Let's look at some of the basic words of the Constitution of the Brothers and Sisters of Charity, the rule our community follows, and apply them to modern living.

> "The Brothers and Sisters of Charity is a Catholic community of singles, celibates, and families called as a monastic and domestic spiritual family into deep love relationships with and in Jesus Christ." (Basic Principles and Vision, Constitution of the Brothers and Sisters of Charity, chap. 1)

Catholic

We are a new monastic community in the church, but we are built on ancient and firm foundations. One of the most ancient is the concept of being Catholic. The word

"Catholic" means "universal" and "full." There is an ecclesial and a personal aspect to this word. On the ecclesial level, St. Vincent of Lerins says that to be Catholic means to believe what the church has always believed since the beginning and what she believes everywhere. It is "universal."

On a personal level, I prefer a nondoctrinal definition. I would like to suggest that it means to be universally filled with Jesus from head to toe, from the inside out. Jesus calls us to an "abundant life." This abundance is a spiritual richness that is found when we divest our old self of self through the poverty of Jesus.

Called

We are called. We did not initiate the universal new monasticism. There is a new monasticism that calls the universal monk within us all. A force greater than ourselves draws us. We were called by Jesus through the Holy Spirit. It is an almost irresistible urging of the Spirit to a life beyond the status quo of any religion. But it fulfills every religion.

I can remember being called by the Spirit when I first read *The Silent Life* by Thomas Merton and having that call confirmed as I visited monastery after monastery. I had the same sense of being called when I heard about St. Francis and the Franciscans at Alverna Retreat Center in Indianapolis. Something wonderful and mysterious was happening inside of me. It was like falling in love, not with a woman, but rather with a specific way of life that fulfilled my every dream and calling in Jesus. It was like discovering what had been within me all along ever since my birth. It was like coming home.

Those called to the universal new monasticism experience something similar, each in his or her own way. Each person must hear the call for himself or herself, but the call is heard in everyone who feels compelled to respond.

Family

Those who hear this call hear it personally, but as soon as we respond we discover that others have heard the same call. We discover a whole new spiritual family. Though we are very different in family and ethnic origins, we all find a common bond with each other because we have all heard the same call from Jesus. The call bridges every human barrier. It is universal.

The monks of old called the leader of their communities an abbot, or spiritual father. This was not to place the abbot in some kind of cultish role but to emphasize that we are indeed a spiritual family. The monastery is a place where spiritual children, brothers and sisters in Jesus, gather together to help one another along our monastic and mystical spiritual way. Yes, we test one another through our human failings and sins, but we support one another through our mutual call to this universal monasticism within each of us.

Monastic and Domestic

This call is not only for those who move into geographic monasteries but also for those who live in their own homes. Some are called to leave their families, their jobs, and their homes to follow Jesus in a completely new environment. Even some families leave everything—except the family God has called them to foster—in order to live in the integrated monastery. But many more hear the call right within their own homes. In the midst of the secular world, they are called to renew the secular world by embracing a monasticism that is hidden. They are in the world but not of the world.

Personal Love Relationship with and in Jesus Christ

In our new monastic community, "personal love relationships with and in Jesus Christ" form the foundation on which our whole way of life exists. We often hear our evangelical brothers and sisters of Christ speak of a personal love relationship with Jesus Christ, and many would correctly say that it is essential to the salvation experience itself. It is certainly basic to our Christian experience and to the new monasticism of Christianity. Each word of this phrase deserves some attention.

Personal

Our relationship with God is personal. No one else can do it for us. Others can pray for us and help us, but we must ultimately make a decision ourselves to give our lives for a higher spiritual purpose through Jesus. It is personal and even intimately private.

Our relationship is personal with a personal God. But what is a "person"? On one level, it is exactly what we think. It is the stuff that makes us who we are. We are not just things or impersonal objects. In Semitic anthropology the spirit, soul, and body are not seen as segregated parts of our human being. They form an integrated whole that we call a "person" or "being."

On another level, person is like the Greek word *prosopon*, or the mask that was used by the actors in the Greek mystery plays. In other words our "person" is much deeper than our mere personality. In fact, our real person is often very different than our personality. Our personality is often the persona we have learned to put on in order to hide from the often difficult and even violent outer world. The sad thing is that we often get confused and think that our personality is our person. We lose touch with ourselves and with everything around us. We end up living an illusion because we do not really even know who we are anymore. Jesus comes to restore us to ourselves. St. Augustine says that Jesus is closer to us than we are to ourselves. He knows us even more than we know ourselves. He comes to restore us to our real person. It is the deepest "us" that makes us who we really are.

God is also personal. He emanates or flows forth into creation. The Father does this through his revelation through creation itself, through the various religions of the world, in a formal way through the Hebrew law and the prophets, and finally through His Son Jesus. He also reveals his person through the various manifestations of the Spirit. The things of his emanations are "knowable" through sense, thought, and emotion. They can be defined in part. We need this in order to know him in the created world of phenomenal existence.

God is also transcendent, or utterly beyond anything in the limited created world. He creates the world as an emanation of his selfless love, and creation reflects his being, but the fullness of his being is beyond creation. He is simply too big to be enclosed in a created form or idea. He is the "Name above all names." His complete being is certainly beyond our human understanding and perception by any of our faculties. So, we can perceive God through our human faculties but only once they have been purified from the false personality, and then only in part.

Love

Our relationship is one of love. There are several words for love in Greek. *Phileo* is the kind of love between friends. As Jesus said, no greater love has anyone than to lay down one's life for one's friends. *Agape* is most commonly used for divine love and means a love that is completely without self-interest but finds itself fulfilled in giving itself completely. *Eros* is where we get our word "erotic" and has sometimes been avoided in Christian usage. But Pope Benedict XVI has taught us that even *eros* was used by the early church fathers to describe a love that was so passionate that it was lifted up above selfish interests to be totally self-giving.

The key to all of this is the word "selfless." Jesus was "self-emptying," according to Philippians 2, and the great "love chapter" of 1 Corinthians 13 says that love does not seek itself. So, real love cannot give in order to get. It gives and finds that it receives the greatest gift when giving without expecting anything in return. Real love never uses people or manipulates them for what it can get out of them.

Relationship with Jesus

We must really "relate" to Jesus. To relate means to have a causal connection between two entities and to account to one another. And we must do this not just once but as a state of life. It is not just relation but a relationship. It is real and ongoing. Many go to church, temple, or mosque to simply "do" religion. That is not enough for the new monasticism. We must actually have a relationship with God. As Christians we do this through the person of Jesus. This relationship is as real as one that we have with the one who is closest to us in the entire world. It is as real, or even more real, than our relationship with a wife, husband, family member, or very best friend. It is that real. But it is even more real than these! Husbands or wives may leave us or pass away. Family members drift away. Friends may come and go. But Jesus remains forever. He never leaves and never dies. Our relationship with Jesus is the most real and longest-lasting relationship we will ever have in all eternity.

Relationships in Jesus

Our love relationship with Jesus includes relationships with one another. It is "with and in Jesus Christ." Sometimes we are only too happy to give up everything and follow Jesus. The problem is that once we do so we look around and wonder who the heck all the other people are! Many of them are not folks we would naturally choose to hang out with. We might think we love Jesus, or at least our idea of him, but we might not like all the other folks much at all. But this is where our love for Jesus is really tested. That is also why community came to be heralded as a basic monastic principle in Christianity. It is also true with the new monasticism today.

Personal relationship with God through Jesus; common union, or communion, with each other in him; and the cross and resurrection as the means and end to that mystical union and communion are from and for which every other discipline that forms our way of life exists. Without the one, the other just becomes vain religion.

Many people think that monasticism is an escape from the unpleasant realities of the church or the world. Many come to our monastery trying to escape the violence of the big bad world, or the shortcomings of the church. No doubt, it is a way to go deeper than the status quo of either. But it is not escape. It is getting to the real core issues that challenge our church and our world today.

The first Christian monks in the Egyptian deserts went there to escape the world in the sense that they were trying to provide an environment for undistracted prayer and meditation. But they also went there precisely because Egyptian myth said that was where the demons that were afflicting the world lived. In other words, they went there to get to the root of the problem of the world, not to run from it! Plus, they had the humility to admit that the problems with the world began with themselves and not with others. They did not run from themselves or from the world. They were trying to solve the problems of the world by getting to the spiritual root of the problems and by beginning with themselves. This is not a bad model for our modern culture that all too often tries to heal only the symptoms, and not society's deeper illness, and usually ends by pointing the finger at someone else by playing the "blame game." The monks of old ruggedly confronted these and have much to teach us in the new monasticism.

If you embrace the new monasticism in order to get away from people in the church or the world, you will find that you simply cannot escape people. They are part of life on planet earth. Plus, trying to escape others is often just an attempt to escape ourselves. I have learned that no matter where I run, I cannot get away from "me." Wherever I have tried to run to get away from the things that bother me most about a person or situation, I seem to repeat it again with another set of people and circumstances if I do not first get to the heart of the problem and solve it in Christ. Those problems are usually within myself and not really so much in others. Often what we dislike in others is our own greatest challenge and is the greatest testing ground for how far we ourselves have grown spiritually.

Jesus Christ

Who is Jesus? This is a question so basic that we might think it out of place in a treatment of monasticism. But we are talking about the "new monasticism," which is found in the Evangelical as well as the Anglican and Catholic traditions of Christianity. It is predominantly Christian but also includes interfaith expressions. So the question, "Who is Jesus?" is important.

Jesus falls squarely into the quasi-monastic and mystical traditions of the world religions. He probably looked and organically "felt" a whole lot more like a Hindu sannyasi, a Buddhist bhikshu, a Taoist or Confucianist sage, a Jewish prophet or Essene, or even an Islamic Sufi than a modern day megachurch pastor, minister, or priest. He certainly has little in common with today's "relig bizz!" In this sense, Jesus complements all the great founders and mystics of the other religions of the world.

On another level, he completes them. He does not do this out of human pride or religious one-upping. He does not fall into the "my religion is better than your religion" syndrome of so many exclusivist and fundamentalist religions seen today. Jesus simply *is* the fullness of the Mystery as found in the

Paradox of the incarnation and the paschal mystery of the cross and resurrection. He does not simply preach the paradox or point to it, though he certainly does both. He *is* the Paradox of paradoxes. He *is* the Mystery of mysteries. This is what makes Jesus unique. So, Jesus satisfies the conservative Evangelical and the progressive interfaith approaches to the new monasticism and harmonizes them in himself.

Jesus was the fullness of God incarnate in humanity. In order to die for another human being, he had to be fully human yet without any sin. In order to carry the debt of all creation, he had to be fully God. Jesus was both. Other religions claim avatars and incarnations. But no other incarnation carries the entire debt of sin, opens a mystical doorway through embracing the paradox and legal fulfillment of the cross, and is raised from the dead to confirm his victory over sin and death. In this Jesus complements and completes all other religions. In this he is unique.

In Hebrew Jesus is called "Jeshua," or "Joshua." This means "savior." The problem is that many of us are religious because we think it is the right thing to do. But in order to follow Jesus we must realize that our life needs saving. We must have reached the end of our rope by trying to do life on our own. To be saved we must realize that we are lost. Today the word "salvation" has probably lost much of its power because we have simply used it so much. It has become casual rather than powerful. It is a lofty ideal rather than an in-the-trenches experience.

I often think that only those who have bottomed out can know what it really is to be saved. In some ways, those who follow a twelve-step program after some form of addiction know more about being saved than the typical church-going Christian. This is deeply personal and emotional stuff. And only those who have gone through it can know what it is all about.

Those in the early monastic tradition were often the ones who had gone through a powerful personal conversion. In later times parents sometimes gave children as an "oblation" to God in a monastery, and these often became solid monks and filled the ranks of large monasteries. But the founding generations of monastic movements were usually made up of people who had been "saved." The new monasticism of today is much the same.

Christ

The word "Christ" means "anointed." Anointed by what or whom? In the Christian tradition we say that the Spirit anointed Jesus. He is "the Christ." A "Christian" means to be "like Christ," or anointed like Jesus.

But what does it mean to be "like Christ"? Sometimes we think that we are anointed, but we are really only excited! It is good to be enthusiastic about God and Jesus and such, but sometimes we mistake mere enthusiasm for the real anointing of the Spirit. Cardinal Suenens gave legitimacy to the Catholic Charismatic Renewal, calling it a source of *enthusiasm in the Spirit*, but John Wesley also once wrote tracts against enthusiasm! There is a balance between the two. When we are anointed we find a wholesome enthusiasm in the Spirit that is much deeper than mere religious excitement. We rediscover its original meaning of being "in God" or "in *theos*."

To be "like Christ" really means to be "like Jesus." We cannot go back to the Holy Land of Jesus two thousand years ago and mimic his culture and time. We are to imitate Christ, but we should not parrot him. That would make a cartoon out of genuine imitation of Jesus. Real imitation of Jesus means to take the universal aspects of Jesus' life on earth and apply it to our culture and time today.

What are these things? Love, forgiveness, mercy, and compassion that go beyond mere law to spirit come to mind. This includes building a world of peace that is built on justice, and a justice that is built on forgiveness. A mystical relationship with God that is truly spiritual is at the root. A willingness to lay down one's life for the benefit of others is its fruit. These are just a few things that come to mind.

The Sermon on the Mount in Matthew's gospel, the love chapter of 1 Corinthians 13, or the self-emptying canticle of Philippians 2 are great Christian Scriptures to meditate on in order to find the character of a real anointed life "like Christ," or "like Jesus." These speak his heart to any who will listen.

But there is another aspect to a life in the Spirit. The Spirit is the very essence of God. In Eastern Christian hesychasm there is a difference between energies and essence. In the West we tend to emphasize essence united with and through energy, but they are still distinct aspects of the whole. God's energies are seen in his emanations in anything that can be perceived about God in the created world through the human faculties of sense, emotion, or thought. This is the realm of doctrine and theology or active ministry. God's essence is within these yet beyond any name, concept, or form perceptible through the normal human faculties of sensations that cause thought and emotion. Pure essence can only be perceived by pure spiritual intuition beyond names, concepts, or forms. This is the place of pure contemplation.

Those who are of the new monasticism are those who are actively open to the things of the Spirit. They must be seekers of the Mystery of mysteries, searchers for the Paradox of paradoxes. The monastic life is one that provides the support of like-minded people who embark on this journey in a very intentional and specific way. We do it in a way that builds on the monasticism of old but is at once both ancient and new.

Monastic

Monasticism is not unique to Christianity. Hindu sannyasi, Buddhist bhikshus, Taoist and Confucianist sages, Islamic Sufis, Jewish Essenes, and holy men and women are all expressions of the monastic religious impetus in humanity.

In historic Christianity, monasticism was the repository of radical gospel living and the mystical expression. Only after it became morally and spiritually bankrupt did the other expressions of consecration surface with the mendicants of St. Francis and St. Dominic, the Carmelites, and then with the societies of apostolic life with St. Ignatius of Loyola's Society of Jesus and those who followed.

The Protestant Reformers brought the radical gospel life back to the average person and pretty much abandoned monasticism altogether. But even then quasi-monastic communal expressions of those interested in giving their life to God remained. Mennonites, Quakers, and the Amish are examples of how even families gave their lives to God in a special way of radical gospel simplicity and mystical union with God.

The cross and resurrection of Jesus remain the highest expression of the radical gospel lifestyle and the mystical union with God it facilitates. And personal love relationships with and in Jesus are what our entire spiritual life as individuals and as a community is all about.

Every religion teaches some basic faith and morality about the spiritual and the divine and about how we are to live as people who follow that spiritual path. These things are objective and to some degree they are logical. But every major religion also teaches a mystical reality that is beyond objective ideas and concepts. This mystical path is best expressed through paradox. A paradox is an apparent contradiction that tells of a deeper and almost self-evident truth. Examples of such paradoxes are finding a spiritual word in silence, communion in solitude, wealth in simplicity, freedom in obedience, and so on. The greatest expression would be finding new life in death, death to the old self. Most folks have had moments of intuitional breakthrough when such truths enlighten them in often life-changing ways.

Monastic life is a way to make an extra commitment to follow a way to such breakthroughs, a way of life supported by others. It can be experienced without the monastic life. But the support of others dedicated to this spiritual path is most helpful and has arisen as a normative expression in most religions. Christianity is no exception.

In the Brothers and Sisters of Charity we say that we have personal love relationships "with and in Jesus." We have a personal love relationship with Jesus, but we also have appropriate love relationships with each other in Jesus. This brings us to the concept of *communio*, or communion, or "common union." This is not only an individual experience of relationship with Jesus. It is personal but also communal. It was this balanced idea that drove the *Pachomian Koinonia* of the first cenobitical monks of the upper deserts of Egypt. *Communio* comes from the Greek *koinonia* and means "community."

Let's look more deeply into some of the basic ideas of the universal monk, the way of a new monasticism.

New

We call this book *Universal Monk: The Way of the New Monastics*. Let's look at some of these words. "New," "universal," and "monk" all beg some basic consideration.

Everything today is "new," improved, or, even better yet, upgraded! I just upgraded my mobile phone and felt that rush of newness as I anticipated the new gadget. No doubt, I will feel a similar rush when the thing arrives. It promises to improve my life by making it all simpler! Yet anyone who has upgraded a computer or cell phone knows that this rush is temporary at best. Within days, or at most weeks, the gadget will become just another utilitarian device used to get work done. The novelty and newness is short-lived. But not to worry! In another year or so, there will be another upgrade that advertising will tell me I "must" have. And if I am not careful, I just might believe them again!

But I am being a bit cynical. There are certainly needs for such upgrades. They do, in fact, help us to get our work done better. The things that we take for granted nowadays were not that long ago considered futuristic gadgets seen only on *Star Trek* and the like. No doubt, as my friends at NASA tell me, the space program did, indeed, have everything to do with developing the primitive core of most of these things. It was up to the wonder-workers at places like Apple to make them a reality in the private world for the rank-and-file citizen.

Today I carry around a laptop that has more power on it than was found on the space shuttles. I have an iPhone that does everything from be a phone to access the internet for e-mail and to play music and movies. I also have an iPad that carries a complete e-book library and accomplishes many of the same tasks as the iPhone and computer. We are in the midst of a technological revolution that is quickly changing the way that we basically function in modern life.

The same is true with the new monasticism. Since Vatican II in the mid-1960s, there have been a plethora of new communities in the church. They are a flowering of the Spirit in the church that is blowing with a fresh spiritual wind. These run the gamut from totally informal with no commitment to fully monastic with traditional vows. They include celibates, singles who can marry, and families, those who live on-site at a community complex and those who live in their own homes. Most of these communities have come and gone. Some have stood the test of time and are still here. And there are still new ones being raised up by the Spirit each year. The living experience of the communities and the oversight of the church help to discern the authenticity of these new communities. It also helps to keep the ones who persevere on course so that they can be vibrant contributors to the ongoing life of the church.

We must be aware of two seemingly contradictory interior problems that most of us carry around. The first is a resistance to change. Most of us hate to be challenged to step out of the safety zones we have constructed in our lives. Some structures of church and community are good. They have been given by God to give us security and are something to prop us up when we are weak. But they can also become a crutch that keeps us from really being healed and walking when God is calling us to step forward. This pattern can be seen especially in older practitioners of any established faith, or monastics in monasteries, but it can also be found in young people who are trying to rediscover fundamentals in their spiritual lives and have gone too far into fundamentalism.

The second is the need for novelty. It can also be found in young people just beginning their spiritual journey and in older folks who have grown tired of the journey they are already on. This is a sort of spiritual consumerism that constantly roams from spirituality to spirituality, movement to movement, and community to community. We will discuss this in greater detail later under kinds of seekers and monks. But briefly it amounts to a spiritual consumerism that ends up destroying both the consumed and the consumer. It is like eating sugar. It gives an immediate spiritual high but cannot nourish. Those who spiritually feed this way are doomed to a pattern of constantly eating but eventually dying from malnourishment. As St. Paul says of such persons, they are always seeking teaching but never come to knowledge of the truth. That truth is right in front of us, and within us, in Jesus Christ all along.

What is needed is a balance between being closed to new ideas and being addicted to them. We need to be firmly grounded in what has come before but completely open to what God is still calling us to step forth into. When this balance is found life becomes a wonderful journey of faith that is both adventurous and secure in faith.

This is really nothing new. Bishop Cordes, when he was in the Pontifical Council for the Laity, wrote a book explaining how each period of authentic renewal and reform in the Catholic Church has witnessed a flowering of new communities raised up by the Spirit. Each major religious family—the Benedictines, Franciscans, Dominicans, Augustinians, Jesuits, and all the rest—is an example of this dynamic. In fact, he submits that any so-called renewal that does not produce new communities must have the honesty to reconsider its spiritual authenticity. This stands as a stark challenge to any renewal today that does not produce good and lasting communities.

Each historic church renewal produces new communities that are unique to its culture and time. But each builds on the wisdom of what has come before. So a very certain development of community styles and spiritualities is seen with the history of new communities in the church. First there were hermits, then those who lived the monastic life in cenobitical community. After these became old and worn–out, in the West came the monastic reforms of the eleventh century with the Cistercians, Camaldolese, and Carthusians. These monastic reforms and the penitential movement paved the way for the mendicants, like the Franciscans, Dominicans, and various Augustinians of the thirteenth century, who saw the world as their cloister and did apostolic ministry among the people as well as lived the contemplative life in monasteries and hermitages. As a result of the mendicant movement, there were not only communities of sisters who lived in monastic enclosure and cloister with solemn vows but also communities that professed only simple vows so that they could leave the enclosure of the cloister and do public ministry among the people. Next came societies of apostolic life who were further freed from the obligation of prayers in common in order to minister alone in the mission field. Moving into the last century came the secular institutes for those who pronounced the evangelical counsels while remaining in the secular world as individuals and came together with other members occasionally. Since Vatican II the new Code of Canon Law allows for both hermits and consecrated virgins who live primarily in their own homes and hermitages but may group together as the Spirit leads. The new monasticism is a further expression of this same movement of the Holy Spirit in our midst.

The Scriptures tell us that we build on the foundation of the apostles and the prophets, with Jesus Christ as the cornerstone, and that we form a spiritual temple made up of living stones. *The Shepherd of Hermes*, an early church writing, extends that metaphor, describing how course upon course is laid on that foundation through each generation and how an angel sent by God ultimately tests each stone. The angel taps each stone with a spiritual hammer. Those that crack and crumble must be replaced. Those that hold together remain in the wall of the spiritual temple of God.

We can extend that metaphor to describe this new monasticism. In each generation we build on what has come before. But we must go into space where no stones have ever been placed before. In order for the wall to remain strong we must build squarely on what has come before. But we cannot go back to the space of the previous stones or we never build the temple up. Those who try to go higher without building squarely on the past are doomed to fall to the ground and break into pieces. Building on what has come before calls us to a progressive conservatism that has the boldness to go even higher. Simply trying to return to the past is a caution against the archconservatives in our midst. And trying to go higher without building squarely on the past is a warning to the radical liberals who want to do something completely new with no real regard for the valid traditions of the past.

My spiritual father and director, Fr. Martin Wolter, OFM, gave another helpful metaphor to me. He explained that the church is like the body of Christ. Like an earthly body the church has a left foot and a right foot. In order for the church to go forward, she must step on both the right and the left foot in succession. At times it may seem that the church is too far to the left or right, but from a broader perspective we can see that she is walking in a straight line. At times we might feel frustrated when the church is on one foot or another. But he encouraged patience, for after one foot will surely come another. Plus, the church is bigger than any one lifetime. We are part of a much bigger spiritual reality on Earth that has a final destination much bigger than what will be reached in our short life span. He said that I could expect the church to change feet two or three times in my lifetime.

This has been my experience so far. When I first became a Catholic, I was most concerned about the far left. I felt like saying, "If you want to become a liberal Protestant, just do it! I will introduce you to the pastor of the church down the street. But don't inflict it on those of us who have actually *chosen* to embrace the beautiful traditions of the Catholic Church!"

Today I feel a bit differently. Today I feel it is the archconservatives who are the scariest of all. Perhaps in an attempt to correct the abuses of the failure of the far left experiment, many young people have embraced an archconservatism that emphasizes the rules and regulations to a fault. Instead of responding to the excesses of the far left, they have reacted and gone to an equally harmful extreme at the other end. Rules and regulations about rubrics, sacraments, church structure, and doctrines will not really save anyone. Only a personal love relationship with God through Jesus in the power of the Spirit can do that. These things are fine insofar as they go. But they only point the way. They are not the way or the spiritual destination. It is important to have a good, dependable map and clear road signs, but they are not the point of the journey. Enjoying the journey and getting to the destination are the point of travel. As I say again and again, the church is not God. It is a gift of God. Liturgy and sacraments and all the like are not God. They are gifts from God that are meant only to lead us back to God. To stay stuck in the gifts is to miss the Giver.

The new monasticism is only about leading folks of every state of life into a relationship with God in a specific and unique monastic way. For Christians this is done through the life and ministry of Jesus Christ. But it can also be very easy to make a god of this new monasticism. In our love and zeal for this new expression in the church and the world, we can get a bit too enthusiastic about what St. Paul called the mere form of godliness and forget the power of it. That power is the presence of God living within us in the Spirit. As St. Paul said, it is no longer I who live, but Christ who lives within me! This is the goal and reason for any new developments in the new monasticism and of the universal monk within us all.

But this does not excuse us from the challenge of the journey. We must be always open for the newness of the Spirit directing us to take the ancient traditions of the church and the monastic heritage and apply them to the culture and times in which we find ourselves. This is very exciting today. More than ever before in any time in history, the world has become the proverbial global village in which those of all faiths, spiritualities, and cultures can dialogue and peacefully coexist and join together to build something truly dynamic in the Spirit of God and the best of our common humanity. The way is not easy. It will take wise discernment and hard work. But the way is now open before us. Those who have the courage and vision to do it can do it. The rewards are enormous. Will you join us? Will you step forward to do something ancient yet new? Will you give your life to become part of the new monasticism, follow Jesus in an exciting and new way, and find that universal monk within us all? I hope that you will.

Universal

We live in an increasingly global world. The far ends of the world are only a computer click away. We speak to each other instantly. We are almost immediately in touch with languages, cultures, and religions we seldom encountered even fifty years ago. We have become a global village. The days of nationalism and parochialism are over. Only a complete collapse in electrical power can stop this technology. And even this would only come after the cross-pollinating of all these factors has already occurred to some extent. This has radical religious implications.

Jesus came into the world to bring salvation to people of every culture, race, and religion. He came to bring a salvation that was "universal" and for all. He completely fulfilled the Jewish religious traditions but surpassed them all. He broke the mold of a religion that was largely tribal to one that was potentially global. His good news was for Jews and Gentiles alike. This was nothing short of radical and is still a cause of consternation among some believers. But Jesus does the same thing to any existing religion on earth. He fulfills and surpasses in a way that values, loves, and respects all that has come before. As the early church grew beyond Jewish population centers, this became particularly pronounced. His message attracted people from all existing faiths of any region. A spiritual revolution was born that shook the world. Today, Christianity remains the largest religion in the world and spans every race, culture, and tongue. Catholicism remains the largest Christian expression.

The word "Catholic" means "universal" and "full." As Jesus says, "I have come that you might have life, and have it abundantly" (John 10:10). In Christian history we have interpreted this, as did St. Vincent of Lerins, to mean "believing what the church has always believed everywhere by everyone." This sounds nice and neat. But in reality it was not so homogenous. Rather, the church went through many struggles in discerning what was orthodox and catholic and what was not. It often came at the cost of arguments that sometimes turned vicious and even bloody. Various interpretations of this "Catholicism" have created many schisms and divisions within the church, the greatest of these being the Protestant Reformation. These created a fracture that ironically and paradoxically blossomed into a rich diversity of expression. But this came at the terrible cost of the unity of the church based on the love and truth of Jesus himself. Unity in diversity sometimes degenerated into simple division that broke unity.

It was from the perspective of this process in the early church that Cyprian of Carthage and Augustine said, "There is no salvation outside the Catholic Church." This idea was spawned by treatments of division and disunity found as early as the Scriptures and the apostolic fathers like Ignatius of Antioch. From one perspective this was logical and even necessary. The church was fracturing into myriad groups with opinions about who and what Jesus was all about. So the appeal to the bishops' leadership as authentic successors to the apostles and their interpretation of the gospel tradition just made good sense. Such an appeal had already been used by the early church fathers, such as Clement of Rome and Ignatius of Antioch, to hold the fledgling Christian community together. It was this appeal that held the early church together and forged her into a major force in the Western world.

Today we face another situation. Today we are not so much unraveling (though some still are!) as coming back together in a regathering toward greater unity. Few are breaking away. Most today are trying to come together. This can be seen in two ways.

First, we have been born into a Christian community that was already divided hundreds of years before us, and we are seeking a reunification of some kind. What the exact expression of that unity might be remains to be seen. But it is clear that it must retain something of the good that each faith community has found. In a word, Catholics are learning from Orthodox, Anglicans, and Protestants, and Protestants, Anglicans, and Orthodox are learning from Catholics. Without denying what is true in our own tradition, we are learning to respectfully listen and dialogue with and, yes, learn from others.

We have also faced the recent sexual abuse scandals that have humbled the once-mighty moral certitude of the Roman Catholic Church. We have had to face an epidemic of ephebophilia (the sexual abuse of underage persons), much of which has found homoerotic expression, by a predominately celibate Latin Rite Roman Catholic clergy. This has called celibacy into fresh question as to its legitimacy. Some have called this the greatest threat to the Catholic Church since the Reformation. Change is in the air, and reform is necessary. New monasticism is offering an integration of celibate, singles who can marry, and family expressions and is addressing this phenomenon without really making it a primary focus. By including all authentic Christian states of life, it is solving some of the problems of focusing too much simply on one.

Second, we are discovering a religious world that is far more diverse than what we have experienced within the Christian tradition alone. It is rich, diverse, and truly global. To simply write off non-Christians as being devious sheep that have climbed into the sheepfold without coming through Jesus is overly simplistic and does violence to true biblical scholarship.

We are learning how to listen, dialogue, and work together with the entire religious tradition of the world as well. This dialogue and work to build a better world makes us all spiritually richer.

Interfaith

On a level that is uniquely monastic, monks of one tradition almost immediately recognize a common brotherhood and sisterhood with monks of other traditions. Be it Christian monks, Hindu sannyasi, Buddhist bhikshus, Taoist sages, Islamic Sufis, Jewish kabbalists, or the holy men and women of primitive indigenous religions, all recognize a common calling that unites them at least on some level. The doctrines and outer forms may differ, but there is something essentially similar within them all that immediately causes one to recognize the other on a level beyond ideas and words. What is this common spirit? I believe it is the search for, and experience of, spiritual Mystery lived out in a lifestyle of renunciation and discipline beyond what is expected or required of the rank-and-file believer of any religious tradition.

This is not to say that all religions are the same or that we can artificially reduce all religions to a syncretistic new one. Indeed, there are seemingly countless religions. Some are good, and some are better. Few are bad. Some are developed, and some are primitive. This must all be considered in religious interfaith dialogue and experience.

Plus, regardless of how much one tries to embrace the religion of another culture, you always do so from your own experience of your own culture and religion. No matter how hard a Christian tries to understand Hinduism, they always do so from a Christian base. It is their life experience and simply cannot be escaped. To try to deny one's religious and cultural base is like trying to deny that the earth is round. It must be considered as part of the equation.

Yet it is true that many in today's world are growing dissatisfied and impatient with the antiquated slowness of established religions to accept contemporary developments. The established religions wisely say that it is not good to move too fast and that it is important to take time to properly discern the spirits. Yet an entire generation is tired of waiting for something better to happen in our lifetime. Meanwhile, the gulf between religion and spirituality grows wider and wider for a growing many. Some are beginning to consider that maybe the time for the established religions has passed and that it is time for new ones that take the best of all and integrate them into a better whole. They believe that it is time for a new day of spirituality instead of mere religion. They believe that a new age is dawning. Of course, the million dollar question is, what does that actually look like, and who is going to lead it?

Jesus, the Only Way?

But didn't Jesus say that he is the only way? Yes, but this is not just a religious incantation of a name, or a "my savior is better than your savior" game. Believing in the real and living Jesus does not allow for a Christian fundamentalism, much less a Christian triumphalism. The name and person of Jesus has content. It has meaning. What does this mean?

I believe that Jesus was probably culturally and spiritually more like a Buddhist bodhisattva or a Hindu sannyasi than a modern televangelist or megachurch pastor. He was a man who completely embodied the mystical as well as the practical aspect of true religion. He followed rituals and respected them but certainly was not unnecessarily bound by them. He simply fulfilled them while transcending them.

Jesus confirms and completes all good religious traditions. He is not a fundamentalist that excludes anything but one's own religion. Nor is he a universalist who says that one religion is as good as another. He says that no one can come to the Father except through him. But this has content. What does this mean?

For the Christian, Jesus is the fullness of God incarnate and the fullness of a human being. He teaches us how to be fully human by rediscovering the divine gift. Other religions also teach that God incarnates himself in various individuals when humanity needs his direct intervention. Avatars are examples of this. But even by their own textual contexts, these tend to be rather partial incarnations and far from perfect in their earthly lives. For example, Krishna taught some extraordinary spiritual things to Arjuna in the Bhagavad-Gita but actually died in a petty squabble between families. The Buddha died from eating bad food. Lao Tzu wandered off out the western borders of China thinking that he was a complete failure. Confucius also died thinking that he had been totally rejected.

Jesus was also rejected and crucified, but he rose from the dead through his divine power and his sharing in the Father's will and the Spirit's power. None of these others rose from the dead. Jesus alone did so. Plus, almost every other incarnation or avatar manifested some faults in his or her humanity. Jesus was tempted in every way we are, but he remained without sin. This is unique among even the incarnation and avatar tradition in other great faiths. For the Christian, Jesus is the fullness of the Word Incarnate.

But we cannot make these claims in order simply to one-up another religion. There are reasons for them, and they can never be made out of religious pride or lack of understanding, love, and respect for another religion. For us, Jesus simply *is* the Paradox of paradoxes. He is such simply by Being and not by trying to outdo any other.

It must also be admitted that Jesus never really preached himself for himself. Bible scholars almost universally agree that the historical Jesus preached change and turning toward a relationship with God as intimately as one knows a loving parent. Jesus preached the Father with the spiritual power of the indwelling Spirit of God. He only preached his own name because he pointed to this relationship in the Spirit more completely than any other teacher. Only later did the apostles and their successors in the church begin to see "Jesus" as a name unto itself for salvation. But even then, Jesus was seen as a doorway from the old and entrenched religions and divisions of the past to a new spirituality that united all peoples of every race, religion, and culture. He is still a doorway to the Father in the Spirit.

But there is another reason why the name of Jesus is powerful and can be seen to be exclusive.

At the heart of the teaching of Jesus is the cross and resurrection. This teaches that there is new life in dying. We find out who we really are by letting go of who we think we are. Jesus says that we must take up this cross daily in order to follow him and that in denying ourselves we find out who we are in him. St. Paul says that we must let go of the old self in order to become a new creation in Christ. He says that it is no longer we who live, but Christ who lives within us.

All of this is mystical and practical. It is a mystical experience found through meditation and prayer and is most practical by changing the way we live every moment of our daily life. We become a constant meditation in every step that we take. As St. Francis said, we should seek not so much to pray but to become a prayer.

The cross and resurrection are a paradox. Most all other religions of the world teach both an objective truth of faith and morality and a mystical truth beyond logic found in paradox. It is found primarily through meditation and prayer. A paradox is a truth that simply *is*. Jesus embodies this paradox in a most perfect way by simply being the I AM. He simply *is*. He *is* the Paradox of paradoxes, the Mystery of mysteries, and the I AM of all other beings.

The Catholic Church teaches that while we might hold the fullness of riches, other faith expressions also possess spiritual and cultural riches. I would add that others might use the riches they have better than we do. So, we can all learn from one another. All religions teach objective truths regarding faith and morality and mystical truths. As Catholic Christians we share much with other religions on many levels. But we hold that Jesus is the fullness of the paradox and the fullness of the Word Incarnate. So, we confirm all that is good in other faiths, but we complete them. We do not do this arrogantly or in a spirit of religious triumphalism. We do this by simply being in the One Who Is.

Jesus, the Eternal and Final Mediator?

Scripture says not only that Jesus' name is the name above every other name but also that his covenant will last until the end of time or the end of this age. In essence Scriptures say that there will be no new New Covenant because there will be no new mediator after Jesus Christ. With this understanding of the final Word, such doctrines as the Trinity, including the eternal second person of God the Son, make great sense, and Jesus' place as the final mediator seems secure.

But this does not mean that our faith is static as individuals, or as a gathered people of God, a church. We are told from the fathers right up to John Paul II that the Holy Spirit brings the church an "eternal springtime." We are "forever young" without being infantile.

In describing the development of doctrine, John Henry Newman portrays the truth of Jesus Christ in the church like the water that flows through a stream. The stream might encounter obstacles that make it look different at various stages of its journey. At some places it is placid and at other places it is turbulent. There are rapids and still pools along the way. The water may seem to change in appearance, being crystal clear at some stages and muddy at others. But essentially it is the same water throughout.

Likewise with the Catholic Church. She has taken on various appearances through the ages. As she encounters various cultures and customs, she adopts some of these by adapting them to the Christian message. She is constantly developing and, from an outward perspective, appearing even to change. But through it all there remains an essential message that can be traced all the way back to Jesus and the apostles.

Jesus and the church might be eternal. But the power of the Holy Spirit certainly does not leave us stagnant. We move through time and space like the water through Newman's stream. We change many external and incidental aspects of how the gospel is lived out and even specifically believed in the church, but there always remains an essential core that does not change. This is the difference between relative and absolute truth. Far more is relative than absolute. Losing the absolute is a great tragedy, and, once it is lost, it is hard to get it back. But far more about that absolute truth has to do with a mystical "reality" than it does a mere objective doctrine, though objective doctrines are necessary in their proper place and should not be lightly jettisoned or set aside. Doctrines develop when we are sure about that essential core, and we can be less resistant to development, and change in the nonessential. When we are not strong in the essentials, we are often very frightened by any change to the externals of the faith in any form.

So as the church moves into a more interfaith era, we must take on a more interfaith aspect that reflects timeless truths in the midst of the space and time in which we find ourselves.

Three Interfaith Models

There are several models for interfaith dialogue. Each contains truth, but not all are equally good. One is the universalist model that says that all religions are pretty much the same and are like separate but equal roads leading up the same mountain. The other is the fulfillment model that says that one particular religion is the only way to the exclusion of others. These two have pretty much proven to be ineffective. One leads to an unhealthy syncretism that loses the unique wealth of each faith. The other leads to an unhealthy exclusivism that leads to the militarism and triumphalism of one faith over another.

The third is the completion model that accepts all the good and beautiful in all religions but sees the completion of all in one's own faith in a way that accepts and includes all. For Christians, this third way is embodied in the way, truth, and life of Jesus in a most powerful way. But we also recognize that others find similar paradoxes in the mystical traditions of their own faith. The only exclusion is when any stand in the way of the Paradox of paradoxes we all point toward, seek, and desire.

The new monasticism embodies a genuine interfaith respect and cooperation. This can happen on the level of bringing godly faith and morality in an increasingly antireligious, secular world. Bringing religious freedom and basic peace and justice throughout the world is a very real area of cooperation with other religions, especially monastics. It also recognizes and encourages the mystical common ground that exists between the monastic expressions of the religions of the world. This can happen through dialogue and shared meditation experiences in a way that maintains the integrity of each one's faith. Monastic Interreligious Dialogue shares the experiences of prayer and meditation with monastics of other religions in a most special way.

Ecumenism

Ecumenism is another level of activity in the new monasticism. Most all expressions of it include non-Catholic

Christians in some important capacity. We are learning from our non-Catholic Christian brothers and sisters, and they are learning from us. They learn that the great richness of the Catholic faith is virtually unequaled elsewhere in Christianity. We learn a great deal from them about the effectiveness of really reaching out to our culture.

Specifically, Vatican II said that non-Catholics have a great tradition of love of Scripture. We also share sacramental life. We recognize the baptismal grace of almost all other Christian traditions. Eucharist is more complex, but we share, to greater or lesser degrees, the various graces that are given by God through our respective communions.

But there is more that has developed in recent decades. Much more. Great Spirit-filled enthusiasm manifested in the Jesus Movement and the Charismatic Renewal between the 1960s and the 1980s. Then there was the Third Wave. Since then a megachurch movement and new worship movement has been witnessed. These megachurches have often been criticized as "consumeristic" Christianity. The new worship music has been criticized as overly secular and shallow in content and style. These criticisms are well-founded in most cases. But simply writing off their success and retreating to our less-than-effective ecclesial safety zones is much like the proverbial ostrich burying its head in the sand. Let's look at some of the positive aspects of them.

When I recently visited the church of one of my good friends in Houston, I was a bit taken aback at first. It seemed like I was entering a Christian mall! First, the church was huge. It included nearly eighty Sunday school classes, the largest of which was a very deep and scholarly presentation of everything from Scripture to Christian history with as many as six hundred attendees. This is unheard of in Catholic parishes!

The hallways were filled with bookstores and coffee shops where top-of-the-line coffee and snacks were available for free! Everywhere I turned genuinely friendly folks made me feel like I was "at home" and helped me find my way wherever I was going. This is unusual at many Catholic parishes.

The worship service was a bit of a turnoff for me, but I cannot help but see its benefits in reaching people of our culture. The music was either a bit manipulative or so loud that I could not hear the singing of the congregants. But I cannot deny that people were actively and energetically involved. Young people want a form of worship that includes their emotional lives. This is rarely found in Catholic liturgies.

The preaching was good in some services and less-than-satisfying in others. The worst example was a Christian motivational speaker/humorist who never really went into biblical and traditional Christian spirituality except for a very shallow presentation of the faith. It was entertaining but not very deep. At best, these megachurch sermons were usually biblical, not overly doctrinal, and energetically called folks into a deeper relationship with Jesus in ways that had great practical impact on their daily lives. It was very good. Preaching is certainly better in Catholic parishes than it was twenty years ago, but we still have a long way to go.

Regarding monasticism, what I said about monastics recognizing each other across interfaith boundaries also applies to ecumenical lines. In particular, many Catholic Christian monks feel an immediate affinity with other Christian monastics. The monasticism of the Christian East has a special place in our hearts, as does its mystical and contemplative experience. We must always remember that division did not formally exist until AD 1053. Since Vatican II, and most especially with Pope John Paul II, and now with Benedict XVI, the Catholic Church has taken on a special mission to reconcile with our Eastern Christian brothers and sisters. Monasticism is a special place where reconciliation can be accommodated through finding common ground in our monastic heritage.

The same can be said regarding more traditional expressions of monasticism in Protestant or interdenominational communions. There are scores of monastic or quasi-monastic communities that adhere to a traditional monastic rule. They come from nearly every denomination. Each of these has its own historical and contemporary context, but there is a commonality in them all. Of course, the most famous of them is Taizé, which is ecumenical by its nature and has a completely new rule of life that builds on the wisdom of all that came before.

But the ecumenical expression also applies to non-Catholic expressions that are not so traditional and may even include married members. Monastics frequently feel a kindred spirit with the Amish or Mennonites. It is of special significance that the group that originally coined the term "new monasticism" is a group of Baptist pastors and their families who are using the Rule of St. Benedict to give their new community the time-tested structure and tradition it needs to avoid meandering off into a communal abyss of directionlessness. Ironically, a monastic charism is seen within these communities that include and are sometimes primarily families.

I am reminded of what St. John Chrysostom said in the early church. He said that whoever renounces the old self for a unique lifestyle within the church to follow Jesus without compromise is a monk, regardless of whether one is celibate or married. He emphasized that Scripture knew of no difference. This cannot be accepted without qualification, but it foretells the new monasticism we are experiencing today and gives precedent that it already existed in the early church in some ancient form.

People of Good Will

The new translation of the Roman Rite of the Catholic Mass restores the use of the phrase "of good will" when talking about all the people on earth. This is most significant. There are many who are not members of any religion but seek God. There are also those who say they do not believe in God but are seekers of good will who search for the transcendent spirituality that underlies human being. They have often been turned off to religion because of the "scribes and Pharisees" in our midst who are most religious but are often far from life-giving spirituality. In a sense, who can blame them for rejecting the version of religion presented to them? I do too, but I reach a different conclusion.

There have been nonreligious monastic expressions in history as well. The philosophical monasticism of the Pythagoreans tried to make an entire way of life out of finding the transcendent through a kind of mathematical universal. Some have speculated that the Therapeutes of pre-Christian Egypt were religious but with a mixture of an atheistic Theravada Buddhism. This seems religious in that Buddhism is normally included as a religion, but, as the Dalai Lama has affirmed, Buddhism ultimately rejects the idea of gods or God. It is really more of a philosophical spirituality.

The new monasticism and the universal monk have a special obligation to bring the light of a vibrant and living spirituality to people of good will who might have rejected God and organized religion today. Perhaps more than any other, monasteries are to be places of a living spirituality in religion that bring an understanding and compassion that draws all people, believers and nonbelievers alike, simply because of the great love they experience there. This is true religion. It is especially what Jesus taught. I am reminded of the great folk legend Pete Seeger, a professed atheist, who has often visited the Bruderhof communities up the Hudson because of the communal harmony and love and great congregational singing he witnessed in their communities.

I am also reminded of when Secretary of State James Baker, a Baptist, spoke to a group of humanitarian agencies years ago.

He said that one of the greatest threats to world peace on the horizon at the time was extreme, fanatical, and fundamentalist religion. By their theological nature they are exclusive, triumphalistic, and militant. They have historically brought hatred and war rather than the love and peace of God, suffering rather than comfort, bloodshed rather than healing. This does not mean that we should not be clear about the fundamentals of our own faith. But some of the fundamentals of any good faith are compassion, tolerance, and love. We need fundamentals without becoming fundamentalist. We need to be rooted and radical but not fanatical. We need a spiritual war against sin within ourselves that brings greater peace and justice to all people of the world.

The new monastics have the great opportunity to be true universal monks today. We simply can no longer afford to shut ourselves into a narrow understanding of our particular religion any more. If we really follow Jesus we must reach out to all people who are willing to join hands with us on any level to help bring peace to this troubled world. Now is the time.

What Is a Monk?

What is a monk? Most of us in the west think of hooded figures who live in imposing medieval castle-like dwellings and chant what is at once beautiful and beyond understanding. Some think of the brown-robed, rope-cinctured Franciscans of the thirteenth century. But there are "monks" from almost every major world religion. They range from the saffron-robed monks of India in Buddhism and Hinduism to the grey-tuniced Zen monks of Korea. Some are almost animal-like in their bare clothing of skins or cotton, and some go "sky clad," wearing nothing but the clothing God gave them at birth. Most are celibate, but some are married, such as the Sufis of Islam, or the Native American medicine men and women. Yet, all these have a similar heart that beats beneath the various religious and cultural externals. And most all of them recognize that kindred spirit in one another despite great differences of doctrine and ecclesiology.

It has been argued that the definition of a "monk" must include celibacy. This is a strong argument. The word "monk" comes from the Greek *monos* and means "one" and "alone." In almost every religion and culture you will find some who renounce sex due to its association with a desire that gives birth to the lust, greed, and power that are at the root of so many of this world's ills. I am reminded of Gandhi, who renounced sexual relations with his wife toward the end of his life, though he never renounced his cohabitation with her. The Dalai Lama feels that this is a great point of commonality between Tibetan Buddhist monks and Christian monks of the East and West. Traditional monasticism is an institutional expression where such renunciation is called for and supported by others of like mind. This is why traditional and canonical consecrated life in the Catholic Church must include celibacy.

But somehow even this definition is too restrictive to catch the spirit of the universal monasticism, especially with the New Monastics. The fire that burned in Gandhi's heart was very much the same as burns within the monks of all religions. The medicine men or women of the Native Americans who went into the wilderness alone to fast and pray on a vision quest understood this universal monasticism, though the word probably never crossed their tongues.

The Plain People also are very kindred to the monastic spirit and charism, though family remains a most important part of their spirituality. We have great friendships with the Mennonites and the Bruderhof, who come from the tradition of Menno Simons, who was a monk before joining the Reformers. Somehow I always feel very much at home when I visit our traditional Mennonite brothers and sisters who live close to our integrated monastery at Little Portion Hermitage.

I am reminded of a funny story of Fr. Benedict Groeschel, one of the founders of the new Capuchin Friars of the Renewal (CFR), when we ministered together at one of the Bruderhof communities on the Hudson River in New York. He said that when they showed him to his room in one of the households and he saw the line of coats and shoes at the entrance, he knew he was in a religious house! While they live differently than we do at the Hermitage, or as he does at his own convent, I shared his sentiments.

The Catholic document on religious life, *Vita Consecrata*, mentions all these expressions of life and adds some clarity. After a sweeping history of consecrated life, John Paul II speaks of new expressions. He first mentions "mixed" communities that include male and female expressions. Then he mentions those that include families and married couples. He recognizes that many of these also pronounce the evangelical counsels that have traditionally been accepted as the defining element to consecrated religious life in the West. But he rightly adds that families do not really fit squarely into the strict category of consecrated life in the West. That remains only for celibates outside of the institution of marriage and free from family responsibilities. But, he does pronounce those outside of traditional celibacy as "praiseworthy," a word reserved by popes historically for endorsement of the way of life. This is not without significance.

The relevant text says:

New forms of the evangelical life

62. *The Spirit* . . . does not cease to assist the Church . . . by *giving new charisms to men and women of our own day* so that they can start institutions *responding to the challenges of our times*. A sign of this divine intervention is to be found in the so-called *new Foundations*, which *display new characteristics compared to those of traditional Foundations*.

The originality of the new communities often consists in *the fact that they are composed of mixed groups of men and women, of clerics and lay persons, of married couples and celibates*. . . . If, *on one hand, there is reason to rejoice* at the Holy Spirit's action, there is, *on the other, a need for discernment regarding these charisms*. A *fundamental principle*, when speaking of the consecrated life, is that the specific features of the new communities and their styles of life *must be founded on the essential theological and canonical elements proper to the consecrated life*. This discernment is necessary at both the *local and universal level*, in order to manifest a common obedience to the one Spirit. In dioceses, *Bishops should examine* the witness of life and the orthodoxy of the founders of such communities, their spirituality, the ecclesial awareness shown in carrying out their mission, the methods of formation and the manner of incorporation into the community. They should wisely *evaluate possible weaknesses*, watching patiently for the sign of results (cf. Mt 7:16), so that they may acknowledge the authenticity of the charism. *In a special way, Bishops are required to determine*, according to clearly established criteria, *the suitability of any members of these communities who wish to receive Holy Orders. Worthy of praise are those forms of commitment which some Christian married couples assume in certain associations and movements.* They confirm by means of a vow the obligation of *chastity proper to the married state* and, without neglecting their duties towards their children, profess poverty and obedience. They do so with the intention of *bringing to the perfection of charity their love, already "consecrated" in the Sacrament of Matrimony.* However, by reason of the above-mentioned principle of discernment, *these forms of commitment cannot be included in the specific category of the consecrated life.* This necessary clarification regarding the nature of such experiences *in no way intends to underestimate this particular path of holiness,* from which the action of the Holy Spirit, infinitely rich in gifts and inspirations, is certainly not absent. . . .

New associations of evangelical life *are not alternatives to already existing Institutions,* which continue to hold the pre-eminent place assigned to them by tradition. *Nonetheless, the new forms are also a gift of the Spirit. . . . The older Institutes . . . can be enriched through dialogue and an exchange of gifts with the Foundations appearing in our own day.*

In this way the vigor of the different forms of consecrated life . . . *will renew faithfulness to the Holy Spirit, who is the source of communion and unceasing newness of life.*

Though only an excerpt, this is a sweeping and beautiful description that retains the integrity of the old while remaining genuinely open to the new. To use the example of musical synthesizers, we are not about trying to confuse definitions or synthesizing differences into a unity based on distorting the purity of acoustic sounds to try to sound like something they really are not. What we are about is an integration that unites many into one while retaining the integrity of each part. It is like a rope or cord that wraps many strands into one stronger thing yet retains the uniqueness of each strand while doing so.

Having said that, there is an intuitive monasticism that defies even the best of Western definitions. It is a universal monasticism of the Spirit. It provides a spiritual home for the universal monk. This book is for a new universal monasticism that is bigger than this strictly Western definition. Many new integrated monastic communities find nothing in the Rule of St. Benedict that cannot be applied directly to married persons living in a more radical approach to intentional community than can be found in the typical parish or parish group. Ironically, the Rule of St. Benedict mentions children in a way that provides some historic reference point for the inclusion of children within an integrated monastery.

"Monk" was first applied to hermits who lived alone. After the example of St. Antony of the Desert, the "father of monks," the word was used when they formed colonies of hermits who gathered in Lower Egypt around a common church and common center where they met on Saturdays and Sundays. A later contemporary of St. Antony in Upper Egypt, St. Pachomius used the word to describe the members and communities that lived in *koinonia*, or "communion," with one another through daily prayer and work together. St. Benedict in the West and Basil in the East also used the word for their communities. Now it is being applied to celibates and couples who seek to follow Jesus in a more intense way. So the word itself has developed through time and has never remained static. It is still developing today.

Let's look further into this tradition that is at once both ancient and new: the monasticism that has rightly been applied at specific points in religious history and is now being applied to our situation today.

Kinds of Monks,
Monasteries, and Seekers

In the thirty some odd years since 1978, we have seen many people come through Little Portion Hermitage. Some are serious; some are just curious. Some are solid as a rock, and some are unstable as shifting sand. They have covered the full spectrum of personalities and mental health. They range from radical to fanatical, mainline to marginal. Through the years we have learned a bit about how to discern the difference and which to receive into the community.

Religion tends to bring out the best and the worst in humanity. Some of the best achievements of humanity have been due to the influence of religion. Also, some of the worst atrocities in human history have been done in the name of God.

Religion tends to attract folks who have been through a conversion. This means that we have often reached a low point, a "point of despair" to bring out our need for God, a "higher power." So we often carry baggage from those experiences. Some have bottomed out through various addictions to chemical substances or destructive behavioral patterns. In our generation it was the proverbial "sex, drugs, and rock 'n roll." For later generations it often included an addiction to money and power or maybe even technology. Once we go through conversion we often continue to carry the mental and emotional baggage of these experiences. We must battle these inner demons for the rest of our lives. Sometimes community is a good place to do that because of the support it gives. Sometimes community relationships become almost impossible because we have not conquered those demons enough to really receive input from others, especially in a more intense community environment.

The more intense monastic approach to community sometimes makes the positive and negative aspect of this relationship dynamic even more pronounced. Monastic community under a rule and abbot make it a testing ground for even the best of individuals. It is a magnifying glass that brings out the best and the worst in the individual's spiritual life. It brings out one's shortcomings to everyone and provides a challenge to either be healed of them or to simply run away. You can run, but you cannot move forward without that healing. It can be very difficult for one who is not really ready for such intense spiritual challenges.

In the tradition of St. John Cassian and the Rule of the Master that predate him, St. Benedict devotes an entire chapter to the various kinds of folks that attempted the monastic life in his day. He describes four different types. Two are good, and two are bad. The good are hermits who live alone after having been trained and tested in community and cenobites who are still being trained in community. He then describes the two bad kinds of monks that were circulating around Europe, the gyrovagues and the sarabaites. He says:

> Third, there are the sarabaites, the most detestable kind of monks, who with no experience to guide them, no rule to try them *as gold is tried in a furnace* (Prov 27:21), have a character as soft as lead. Still loyal to the world by their actions, they clearly lie to God by their tonsure. Two or three together, or even alone, without a shepherd, they pen themselves up in their own sheepfolds, not the Lord's. Their law is what they like to do, whatever strikes their fancy. Anything they believe

in and choose, they call holy; anything they dislike, they consider forbidden.

Fourth and finally, there are the monks called gyrovagues, who spend their entire lives drifting from region to region, staying as guests for three or four days in different monasteries. Always on the move, they never settle down, and are slaves to their own wills and gross appetites. In every way they are worse than the sarabaites.

It is better to keep silent than to speak of all these and their disgraceful way of life. (RB 1.6-12)

We have certainly encountered versions of these latter two kinds of monks described by St. Benedict in our own day. This is true in traditional monasteries but perhaps even more frequent in expressions of the new monasticism due to the novelty of its expression. Those who have been clearly found to be unsuitable for life in a traditional monastery often hold out hopes that new monasteries will embrace them due to their need for new membership. In most recent years, however, I have noticed that even a few traditional monasteries have sometimes begun accepting more marginal individuals due to their need for vocations in the midst of the recent vocational crisis. This is a problem wherever it occurs.

Today there is no end to individuals who wander from place to place trying to find acceptance yet unwilling to change their own patterns that might make that acceptability impossible. Many wear a monastic habit of some sort but really do not live in obedience to anyone, be it the church or a real spiritual or monastic superior. At first blush these individuals may seem quite spiritual and charismatic, but when placed within the environment of community relationships, that spirituality and charisma are tested and found to be wanting through the continued evidence of non-refined ego and self-will under the guise of spirituality and charismatic gifts. These folks rarely last long in a genuine monastic community setting.

We have seen families come through who lived in busses and tepees and others who rode in Lexuses and high-end motor homes. We have also seen pilgrims in all kinds of monastic garbs. I think that we have seen the habit, scapular, hood, and veil put together in every way and color conceivable! Some are legitimate pilgrims and seekers. Some are frauds. Some are just weird. Some wear the garb but indulge in substance abuse and talk way too much.

Some are true people of holiness and prayer. They have always been a blessing to our community. I remember one such pilgrim who walked with his donkey to Our Lady of Guadalupe in Mexico City and stopped at Little Portion along the way. We made his donkey some felt boots to walk on the rocky Arkansas dirt roads. We heard that he later also walked across Europe to the Holy Land, but his dear donkey had given up the ghost! He was a true man of prayer who talked little, worked hard, and prayed more than most of us.

There has also been no shortage of new monastic groups, especially since the time of Vatican II and the ensuing renewal throughout both the ecumenical and Catholic expressions of the Christian faith. Most of these have come and gone. Only a few have persevered. Most of those who have come and gone did not live under a clear religious rule of life and in obedience to a religious superior within their community and the greater expression of the church. Groups like these are almost always destined to disintegrate through lack of cohesiveness in vision and humble submission to tangible expressions of it through a written rule and established spiritual leadership.

In the eleventh century there was a spiritual reform within religious life in Western Christianity. It is often called the Gregorian Reform. The Spirit raised hundreds of new communities up in the church. Most of these came and went. A few persevered and still exist today. The Camaldolese, Carthusians, and Cistercians are perhaps the best known within the monastic history in the West. The Camaldolese and Carthusians were semi-eremitical expressions trying to rediscover the charism of the first monks and hermits in Egypt. The Cistercians were a cenobitical reform attempting to return to a more true and primitive expression of the Rule of St. Benedict.

The Camaldolese, in particular, often encountered preexisting groups of hermits and monastic communities and brought them under the Rule of St. Benedict and an abbot. Some writers have said that between St. Romuald and St. Peter Damien over one hundred communities were either reformed or founded. Some of these were older communities that needed a renewal in the Spirit, and some were newer groups that needed to be given some sense of order and direction.

Blessed Paul Giustiniani did something similar in a reform of the Camaldolese community during the time of the Reformation and Counter-Reformation. He mainly encountered preexisting small groups that were living without a religious rule or clear leadership. He gave them the Rule of St. Benedict and a reformed constitution of a more strictly semi-eremitical expression of the Camaldolese.

Also of interest is the thirteenth-century mendicant expression of St. Francis of Assisi. These mendicants were little brothers who attempted to live the gospel of Jesus Christ literally. As such, they had "no place to lay their head." They did not at first live in monasteries but wandered the countryside living in abandoned caves or huts in which they prayed and ministered among the people according to their gifts and talents. Very soon they began to establish hermitages just outside the villages of Italy in which they ministered. One of the first written documents of St. Francis of Assisi is his so-called Rule for Hermits. And early biographers and journalists often say that the brothers lived in hermitages at night and throughout some of the day and ministered by doing lowly tasks among the people during part of the day.

This new expression of religious life in the thirteenth century could easily have been considered one for gyrovagues and sarabaites. In many ways they fit the description well. But there are two things the first Franciscans had that kept them from lapsing into this traditionally recognized abuse of monasticism. They had a clear commitment to a written religious rule and a religious superior duly recognized by the Catholic Church.

Today is no different. The new monasticism encounters all the same challenges of new monastic expressions from times past, including a wide variety of types of individuals that knock on the monastery door. These range from radical to fanatical, marginal to mainline, healthy to unhealthy. And like the monks of old, expressions of the new monasticism have had to discern the difference between truly Spirit-led individuals and those who are still ego-driven under the guise of spirituality.

New monastics also face the challenge of establishing a good structure for their way of life. Many new communities fail because they do not establish a good rule, constitutions, and leadership structure for their otherwise charismatic experience. We were most blessed by having several Franciscans and a Cistercian Benedictine who helped us establish good communal structures of leadership, church constitutions, and secular legal incorporation that ensured a healthy system of checks and balances for our leaders and members. Once established, obedience becomes easier, and extremes that have cultish tendencies are better avoided. I remember one elder from the Anabaptist tradition who conceded that he envied that our community exists under the authority of a larger apostolic church instead of being completely on its own as a church unto itself. I am immensely grateful to those friars and monks who helped us in the beginning and to the many bishops, abbots, clergy, and religious who have helped us ever since. Even with this help the road has been challenging at the very least. I cannot imagine trying to make it without the help of this larger sacred church and monastic tradition.

For many seekers on the personal level, finding the right community is not so much a matter of good or bad but of good and better. For many others it's not even a matter of good and better but of simply finding the right place to live our God-given calling in today's world. Many of the individuals who do not "work" in more intentional expressions of new monasticism can appropriately associate with monasteries and live as healthy and productive participants in local parish life. For them it does not mean that they have failed at monastic life but are simply made to succeed by living a monastic spirituality in the world within the context of the parish, their families, and the secular work environment.

It is our experience that living within an actual monastery is most difficult for the average American. Being associated with the monastery is simply more livable for most in today's environment. Living within the monastery requires a voluntary relinquishment of one's self-will and self-determination under a rule and leadership that simply runs counter to the American ethos. America was founded on the principles of escaping big government and authoritative religious leaders in order to have both political and religious freedom. We are a culture of rugged individualists, which still prevails across America to greater or lesser degrees. So the notion of giving up that freedom, albeit freely and voluntarily, is difficult for most of us. As I often said when ministering in Texas, we want to benefit from monastic spirituality but don't want to actually join monasteries because we don't want to "give up our truck!" Whether we live in Texas or not, this same sentiment is found throughout the United States.

For most folks, associating with monasteries, but not actually joining them, is the most attractive thing to do. There is a huge rise in the numbers of oblates, seculars, and associates of religious communities in the last ten years. The ratio of associates to monastics is ten to one, and in some cases fifty to one. In the Brothers and Sisters of Charity we call them "domestics" based on the word "domicile" or "home," and we apply this term primarily to those who live in their own homes throughout the world. We have seen a dramatic rise in the numbers of those who are joining this expression of our community.

Many say that a real rise in numbers of actual monastic membership will only come when the secular world in which we live becomes so hostile to authentic Christian living that we will need the daily support of other like-minded Christians to persevere in our faith.

Perhaps due to this dynamic there are many intentional expressions of actual new monastic communities in Europe today. Serious Christians in Europe often gather in more intense expressions of intentional community to provide the mutual support needed to maintain a more radical but not fanatical approach to gospel living in the midst of an environment that is often hostile to serious religious expression. Plus it has been observed that even Western Europeans are more community-oriented than average Americans. We Americans tend to be rugged individualists. This makes community more difficult for us.

This individualism has some historical causes that involve the understanding of the role of government in daily life. In general, Europeans have a much more positive view of government. In Europe, government saved the people from lapsing into barbarianism after the fall of the Roman Empire. Monasteries and the church played no small part in this dynamic. Many Europeans have a kind of societal DNA that allows them to see government and communal structures as a positive savior from the terrible destructiveness of barbarianism.

Eastern colonial America was formed as an experiment to escape the intrusion of large government into daily life, including religious freedom. America was formed on the premise of keeping government to the bare minimum necessary for basic functioning. The role of the individual was most important as thousands homesteaded into the western wildernesses. For us, community is important but takes on a far less intrusive expression in the freedom of the individual on both the secular and religious levels.

Today the governments of Europe are becoming more intrusive and even hostile toward religious expression in the public forum than ever before. Within this generation some would say that they are trying to rewrite religion out of their histories in an attempt to further secularize. Pope Benedict XVI is addressing this reconstructionist approach to the rewrite of European history by the European Union by continually pointing out the marriage of European history with Christianity. It remains to be seen how effective he will be.

Against this backdrop we are witnessing many new expressions of the new monasticism in Europe today. My wife and I recently attended a Congress of New Consecrated Communities in Rome that included many representatives of large and small communities being raised up by the Spirit in the church today. Most of these were from Europe. Only two communities, including ours, were from North America. All included not only those who associate with monasteries but also those of all states of life who actually join them.

We do not see great success in people who join actual monasteries in America at this time. In America today we still exist under the external structures and moral guise of Christianity. But under that veneer is a society that is quickly secularizing and even paganizing. This can often be hostile to traditional Christianity. In that environment new forms of monasticism can prove most helpful to individuals who want to radically but not fanatically follow Jesus and live the gospel in the modern world.

But even in the less externally intensive expressions of associating with the new monasticism we still encounter unhealthy patterns of spirituality that are not helpful to the group. Fanaticism, rather than authentic radicalism, is a great problem in the religious expression of neoconservatism today. Likewise, the "joiner syndrome" of those who migrate from religious group to group can be counterproductive to the stability needed to really establish a fruitful community of any kind. As a sign on a pastor's wall I once visited said, "We want spiritual fruit, not religious nuts!" This certainly holds true for the new monasticism as well.

The new monasticism is finding ways to legitimately integrate different personalities and spiritualities into one alternative gospel community living alongside and counter to modern culture. The traditional types of monks spoken of by St. Benedict and the entire monastic tradition can be most helpful in finding a starting place for that process and the discernment of the individuals called to the various expressions of these new monastic communities. They provide ancient wisdom that is still relevant when adopted and adapted today.

Solitude and *Monos*

Most of us do not live in solitude. We spend most of our life in the companionship of a spouse and children within our families and then in rather close proximity with others during our work time. Even in church we are elbow to elbow with other people in the pew. We live in a very busy and crowded society. Often many people feel that the only time they have alone is commuting back and forth to work in their car!

Yet, all of us have a need for solitude. It is part of the human condition. It's part of how we are made. Solitude is part of the truth, the reality, of our human being. All of us know the paradoxical truth that we find mystical communion in solitude. We have all experienced it in the solitude of nature, or even within our private room, or on a warm summer night in the privacy of our own backyard. Anyone who is fully human has experienced this intuitive breakthrough to some extent. It is a truth beyond mere logic. It's the truth that is mystical and intuitive; it is a truth that is self-apparent on the level of our deepest being.

Different people experience this in different ways. Some are introverted. Others are extroverted. Ironically, even the extrovert often has need for solitude. What constitutes the difference between the introvert and extrovert is not the need for solitude but how one processes reality. The introvert might be very outgoing in a crowd but processes the reality of what occurred in the crowd by withdrawing from it and processing it inwardly. The extrovert might well enjoy times of solitude and silence but can process the reality of what occurs in a crowd while still in the midst of the crowd. Many years ago a Myers-Briggs counselor told our community that many people within contemplative cloisters of religious life actually test out as extroverts rather than introverts. This is because there is still a great social element even to the cloistered contemplative life. But even extroverts need solitude. Most people have a need for both social interaction and solitude for a balanced life.

Monastic life is an institutional response to that need. Either as colonies of hermits or as strict communities of cenobites, monasteries provide a religious framework for the human need for a balanced life of community and solitude.

As we have discussed, "monk" comes from the Greek *monos*, which means "one" and "alone." Solitude is basic to the universal monk, even to one who lives out in the world. But Scripture also says, "it is not good that the man lives alone." So we are talking about a healthy solitude, not an unhealthy isolation. As Evagrius said, the monk is one who is "separated from all, and united with all." Monks go into solitude to find greater "communion," or "common union," with God and everyone and everything in God's creation. This monastic reality requires physical solitude but is essentially something quite mystical and spiritual.

The writings of the early Desert Fathers are replete with admonitions to "flee the world." In fact, some of the sayings of the Desert Fathers would indicate that their salvation depends on it. This has been a cause for criticism throughout the centuries and most especially in our recent history. Indeed, if the monks were simply running away, the criticism would be well-founded. Solitude can never be an escape from reality. It must be a confrontation with the ultimate reality of God, creation, and our deepest self.

A proper understanding of the Desert Fathers of Christianity indicates that they were not running from reality at all. They were embracing it! Early Christian monasticism is a phenomenon of the Spirit raised up from the desert of Egypt. In Egyptian mythology of that time the average person believed that the demons lived in the deserts. So, if the monks perceived a social and spiritual problem within the great cities of Egypt such as Alexandria, they believed that in order to get to the core of the problem they had to "flee to the desert" to solve the deeper spiritual problems of greater civilization. So they were not really running away at all! They were entering the field of spiritual battle. They were not running from the problem. They were going to the heart of it. They were not escaping it. They were really solving it.

But the monks had no illusion about blaming others for society's ills. They did not go to the solitude of the desert to fix "you." They had the humility to begin with themselves. They started by retiring into solitude for a face-to-face encounter with themselves and God. They had a stark encounter with the truth within themselves. There were no distractions of social life to create "ambient noise." It was pure social silence and stillness. There was no place to hide. They either faced this reality down or fled back into the activity of the world in order to mask and run from this reality.

The monastic regimen was an intensive understanding of how virtue and vice work within the human psyche. As time unfolded, a system of eight vices developed, complete with the psychological and spiritual understanding of what gave rise to them and how to combat them in ways that were both practical and mystical. These eight vices began with little external and internal things such as gluttony, the need to control, or self-preoccupation, and ended with actions that were most harmful to oneself and to others. It was from this list of eight vices that the seven deadly sins were formulated, first by the abbot near St. Catherine's Monastery on Mount Sinai, and then by St. Gregory the Great. Today, commentators marvel at the psychological insight of these primitive desert monastics.

This is a great lesson for us to learn today. So often we have a tendency to blame others for our own problems. If we watch the news channels, the airwaves are filled with blaming public figures for their many failures while we remain most lenient with ourselves and unwilling to take responsibility for our own failings and shortcomings. Programs such as Alcoholics Anonymous have been most successful in encouraging people to take responsibility for their own behavior, regardless of what others have or have not done to them. We may rightly realize the environment that helped give rise to our behavior, but we must all eventually take personal responsibility for the decisions that brought us to our current situation in life. As St. Paul said in his letter to the Galatians, we can pray for one another and "bear one another's burdens," but in the end, "everyone must bear their own burden." In other words, we must all take responsibility for our own actions. The monks of old teach this lesson very well.

Solitude is the environment where such self-awareness can be developed and purified. By clearing away the external noise and clutter on the sensual levels of sight, sound, taste, and touch, we can better focus on what is really going on within.

For the monks the cell is the place of solitude. The cell is the place where heaven comes to earth. The words "celestial" and "cell" have the same root and mean the place where heaven comes to earth. The cell is the concrete environment in space and time where one can practice both solitude and silence. The word came to be applied not only to the individual hermitage but also to groups of hermitages or entire monasteries called "kellia" or "the kellion." St. Francis of Assisi eventually extended the whole notion of the hermitage and the cell universally, saying, "The world is my cloister, my body is my cell, and my soul is the hermit within." But he never did away with the need for an actual time and place for solitude and silence. Indeed, almost all the places he founded were hermitages. From there he ministered to the entire world. Authentic ministry flows from solitude and leads back into solitude. It is there that union with God is found.

The Desert Fathers said succinctly, "Go sit in your cell, and your cell will teach you everything (Abba Moses)." In the eleventh century St. Romuald said similarly, "Go sit in your cell like a chick, and empty yourself completely."

St. Anthony the Great said, "Just as fish die if they stay too long out of water, so the monks who loiter outside their cells or pass their time with men of the world lose the intensity of inner peace. So like a fish going towards the sea, we must hurry to reach ourselves, for fear that if we delay outside we will lose our interior watchfulness."

He continues: "He who wishes to live in solitude in the desert is delivered from three conflicts: hearing, speech, and sight; there is only one conflict for him and that is with fornication."

Even in cenobitical monasteries where monks live a more intensely communal life, solitude is most important. It is said that cenobitical communities live alone together.

As the Rule of St. Benedict says in chapter 66, "The monastery should, if possible, be so constructed that within it all necessities . . . are contained, and the various crafts are practiced. Then there will be no need for the monks to roam outside, because this is not at all good for their souls" (RB 66.6-7).

In the thirteenth century St. Francis of Assisi also emphasized the importance of the hermitage where a handful of brothers would live in solitude together. For St. Francis this meant that one or two would live in strict reclusion for a period of time, while the other one or two would take care of their daily needs. Those who took care of the active needs of the little community were called the "mothers." Those who lived in strict reclusion were called the "sons" and were taken care of by the mothers. As the Spirit led them, they would exchange roles between the active mothers and contemplative sons. Most scholars believe that they met together for common prayer on a daily basis. But, a true integration between solitude and community was established.

The entire monastic tradition is based on nothing other than the Gospel of Jesus Christ. Jesus was alone in solitude during his temptation (Luke 4) and "often withdrew to deserted places to pray" (Luke 5:16). He often took three of his closest disciples with him, however, into greater solitude. Peter, James, and John were with him in solitude before the transfiguration (Matt 17), or his agony in the Garden of Gethsemane (Matt 26:36-46).

The new monasticism has tended to integrate all of these traditions into one. The average new monastery is an integration of solitude and community, of hermitage and cenobium. Usually this means allowing ample time for individual privacy and communal prayer and activity. It also means allowing individuals time in greater solitude in specific places set aside as hermitages around the common buildings of the monastery.

Many solitaries living in the desert have been lost because they lived like people in the world. Matrona said, "It is better to live in a crowd and want to live a solitary life than to live in solitude and be longing all the time for company." Many bring the world into their solitude, not as prayer, but simply as a distraction from prayer. Instead of releasing everything to God in solitude, they simply end up obsessing about the problems of the world and desecrating their gift of solitude. This is not the way and can be far more harmful than simply going out into the world with the love of God.

I would caution against false solitude. In our short history we have seen all kinds of folks seeking solitude. Because we call ourselves a "hermitage," we get many folks who think they want to be hermits. Some are sincere but do not really know the sheer terror that extended solitude can bring as one faces the naked reality of one's soul before the all-knowing God. In solitude there is simply no place to hide and not much to distract you from that naked encounter of the alone with the Alone. Others are just playing at being hermits and monks. They use solitude as an excuse to simply get out of work and the responsibility of working relationships with others. This never works. It is false solitude. Those who are seeking only to play with solitude in this way are rudely awakened when they visit us and we assign them to work on the farm for six or so hours a day. As Prior Bruno once told me at New Camaldoli in Big Sur, "The young dreamers come here wanting to spend all their time in solitude. Then, we send them into the bakery to bake bread!" Only if they are faithful in community for ten or so years do we allow them greater solitude. They often move on pretty quickly. But we do have some who stay for longer periods of time in hermitage. It is possible for the ones who are truly called and faithful.

For our domestic members, or what other communities might call oblates, seculars, or associates, this means spending some daily time in solitude and silence within one's own home, in nature, or in a sacred space. We generally encourage people to spend a twenty- to thirty-minute period of time daily in silence in a space set aside specifically for this purpose. It might be a prayer room or prayer corner in their house. Where weather permits it might be a space outside. Or it might be a daily trip to a monastery or church. What's important is that some solitude and silence are experienced in a qualitative way on a daily basis.

For most people this will be a sacred space within their own home. We recommend keeping the space there simple, neat, and clean. A simple crucifix, an icon or two, and a candle will help to focus on sacred things. Otherwise this space should be quite simple and uncluttered. In the case of a prayer corner, some of our domestic members find the use of a swivel chair that can turn toward a living room during social times and around to the prayer corner for private prayer times an efficient use of more limited space. For those who can, a prayer corner or even an entire room set aside for solitude and silence is ideal.

It's not easy to carve out a space for solitude or the time for silence in the midst of today's busy and frenetic schedules. But it can be done! If we can take time for special social engagements and dinners, then we can certainly take time to devote to the one with which we have the greatest relationship in all the universe: God. It is from this relationship that all other relationships flow and find their meaning. If we can take time for one, then we most certainly can, and even must, make time for the other.

So make the space for solitude in your life, and you will find great communion with every other person and thing in creation, humanity, the church, and with God himself. Rather than isolating you, it will connect you with everything important in your life. But rather than only being connected in a superficial and stressful way, it will connect you in a way that brings life and health to all. This is the lesson of solitude.

Silence and Speech

I remember one of my first visits to the Basilica of St. Francis in Assisi. The place is utterly gorgeous and awe inspiring. Most people keep a healthy silence, but things being completely tourist as well as pilgrim, they lapse into talking after the initial awe. The noise in the lower church tends to slowly swell until it starts to become more like a shopping mall than a church. At that point one of the good Italian friars yells out, "Silencio!" Immediately, the place falls into a completely stunned silence, and the whole process begins again. This repeats about every fifteen minutes or so.

This is a pretty good analogy for the place of silence and speech in life. We enjoy silence, but we tend to talk a bit too much. From time to time, we need a good shock to call us back to the silence again. But we should not be too surprised by this need for it or the tendency away from it. It is all part of being human.

We live in a world of almost constant noise. People seem to be talking "at" us all the time. The news screams its agenda. Commercials try to impel us to buy their products. Everyone tries to convince us. Then there is the internet. Though using the keyboard, people are talking all the time. It seems incessant. Even as I write this chapter on silence from my hermitage, my e-mail dings for me every couple of minutes. People are talking more and more, yet we communicate less and less. Ironically, silence teaches us how to really communicate from our soul and spirit. But we often have to be silent and still in order to hear those deeper realities.

Here at Little Portion Hermitage we value silence deeply and have places and times for it. We sometimes have to remind ourselves about it, especially since many are new to this way of life. We even used to consider that since we broke silence so much, maybe it was an unrealistic ideal that should be dropped. But, without exception, every time we considered this option, it was unanimously voted down. We need silence. It is one of the main reasons why most of our members came to a monastery in the first place. It is also a need for the universal monk, even when we live out in the midst of the noise of the secular world.

There is a common misconception about monastic silence. Most folks think that monks take a vow of silence. This is not, and never has been, the case. Even in the most extreme expressions of silence, such as with the Cistercians, there were always periods of time when speech was possible. In the monastic tradition silence has never been an end unto itself. It has always been a means to an end. That end is to be able to hear the word of God more clearly and to speak more charitably and effectively to one another.

The Desert Fathers give us a clear indication that silence and speech worked together. The *Institutes* and *Conferences* of St. John Cassian give us ample proof of monks coming together to confer with one another about the monastic life. The *Sayings of the Desert Fathers* are themselves the collected conferences of elder monks with younger disciples and brothers. All of this implies that the monks met together frequently to talk about their monastic life. Thus, silence was not an end unto itself, and speech was an important part of sharing the values of monastic life with one another.

This is not to say that silence was not valued highly among the first monks of the Egyptian deserts. It is said of Abba Agathon "that for three years he lived with a stone in his mouth, thereby he had learned to keep silent." This clearly indicates how seriously the Desert Fathers took the discipline of silence. And I must admit that there have been times when I wished a similar custom was still practiced with some monastics today!

But they certainly did not hold it to be absolute either. The story is told of Abba Arsenius: "Once Arsenius came to a place where there was a bed of reeds shaken by the wind. He said to the brothers, 'What is this rustling noise?' They said, 'It is the reeds.' He said to them, 'If a man sits in silence and hears the voice of the bird he does not have quiet in his heart; how much more difficult is it for you, who hear the sound of these reeds?'" In other words, silence must be not only an external reality but also an internal one.

St. John Climacus tells a similar story. He adds that a brother moved from the coenobium of the community into a hermitage and was actually angered by the sound of the wind through the reeds. So he had created an environment of silence but had not learned to silence the anger within his own soul and achieved nothing in the end.

Such stories ring true for anyone who lives in monastic community. There are always those who are scrupulously silent but carry around an inner anger that makes them appear much more like religious volcanoes than like peaceful contemplatives. No one dares disagree with them or upset their "holy" routine. I have often said that some charismatics are just excited and some contemplatives are just passive aggressive!

St. Bernard says that balance is what is necessary and can be discerned in something as simple as how a monks walks. There are those who loudly stomp around and swing their arms wildly as if to announce their presence wherever they go. And there are those who creep around in a sickeningly pious self-deferential silence, as if to announce their humility before everyone for praise. But Bernard says that a real contemplative finds a certain naturalness in his or her gait that is neither hurried nor unnaturally slow. It is easy and natural. It is not for show but simply flows from a balanced and healthy spiritual life. Thomas Merton maintained that you could tell a lot about a brother's spiritual life by simply observing how he opens and closes a door.

The Rule of St. Benedict brings this together in a balanced moderation regarding silence. Interestingly, there is no chapter titled "Silence" in the Rule of St. Benedict. Rather, chapter 6 is titled simply "Restraint Of Speech." This implies a relation between silence and speech rather than silence in and of itself.

Chapter 6 begins with a strong affirmation of the value of silence by quoting Psalm 38. It goes on to say, "Here the Prophet indicates that there are times when good words are to be left unsaid out of esteem for silence. For all the more reason, then, should evil speech be curbed" (RB 6.2). It recognizes that learning this discipline is not always easy. Consequently, the monk is placed under the guidance of an elder or spiritual father in learning this discipline. It says, "Indeed, so important is silence that permission to speak should seldom be granted even to mature disciples. . . . Speaking and teaching are the master's task; the disciple is to be silent and listen" (RB 6.3, 6).

The Cistercian reform of the eleventh century continued in this tradition by returning more radically to it after the monks had strayed from it in the centuries following the establishment of the Rule of St. Benedict. It was only many centuries later that a reform of the Cistercians by de Rancé at La Trappe, popularly called "Trappists," used sign language more universally. But even then speech was not completely forbidden. Probably the greatest modern example of Cistercians is Thomas Merton, who originally joined a Trappist expression of their community. Today, the various historical reform movements of the Cistercian Benedictine family have been consolidated into what is simply called "Cistercians of the Strict Observance." In the Strict Observance silence is still valued as a precious part of their tradition, but appropriate speech is allowed and even encouraged. Silence is not a goal unto itself.

Even in the more apostolic mendicant tradition of the Franciscans, there is a balance of silence and speech. The Rule of 1221 says, "far from indulging in detraction or disputing with words (2 Timothy 2:14) the Friars should do their best to avoid talking, according as God gives them the opportunity. . . . They are to speak evil of none (Titus 3:2); there must be no complaining, no slander; it is written, 'whisperers and detractors are people hateful to God.' (Romans 1:29). And let them be moderate, showing all mildness to all men (Titus 3:2), without a word of criticism or condemnation; as the Lord says, they must give no thought even to the slightest faults of others (Matthew 7:3; Luke 6:41)."

In his so-called Rule for Hermitages, Francis encourages silence but also allows time to talk to the "mothers," who care for the needs of the contemplative "sons." Even out on ministry he cautions against too much talking and encourages only reverent and respectful speech. In other early sources, he goes so far as to say that even motivational preachers should avoid speaking in ways that draw too much attention to themselves. Their words are to be "examined and chaste." They are also to be "brief, . . . Because the Lord himself kept his words short on earth." Thomas of Celano says that they "Hardly spoke even when necessary." He says that the Poor Ladies of San Damiano (later called the Poor Clares) kept silence so intensely in their monastery that they almost forgot how to speak when they actually needed to. This is an obvious exaggeration, but it shows how important silence was to the early Franciscans.

In the new monasticism, our community also encourages a healthy balance of silence and speech. In our noncanonical Way of Life we say that we make a covenant of substantial silence. We profess "Substantial Silence: to live a life with an attitude of humble silence so that others might hear the living word of the gospel of Jesus Christ."

Again, silence is most important, but it is not an end in itself. We value silence because it clears the mind and the emotions so that we can better hear the word of God for ourselves. Having better heard the word of God for ourselves, we can speak it more lovingly and clearly to others. It even allows us to silence the good things that we might say but that might not be the right thing at the right time, so that only the best thing might be said. Simply put, it means that we speak less but say more.

In order for silence to really be active in our life we have to provide the right environment to establish it and to protect it. This means that there must be times and places for silence. Some of those times and places are private, and some are communal.

For instance, we keep the traditional Grand Silence from the end of Night Prayer, or Compline, until the beginning of Morning Prayer the next morning. Since we pray Night Prayer privately this means that anywhere from eight o'clock to ten o'clock in the evening until the beginning of Morning Prayer at a quarter to seven the next morning we keep an absolute silence, except in extraordinary circumstances where charity demands that we speak.

After Grand Silence we keep substantial silence until noon every day. This means that we may speak, but we try to keep an attitude and spirit of silence throughout the monastery. In other words, we speak when necessary but remain silent otherwise. It also means that when we speak we try to do so in subdued tones so as not to disturb another's prayerful silence.

In some ways this is unnecessary in older monastic communities that are more practiced in the ways of silence. Once we visited the Cistercian monastery of Assumption Abbey in

Ava, Missouri. When we asked them if they kept particular times of silence they responded that such a discipline was unnecessary in their monastery. They kept substantial silence at all times but were free to speak whenever speech was truly necessary. Perhaps due to our youth as a community, it's necessary for us to engage in this as an intentional discipline at particular times so that it might become more normal for us at all times.

Substantial silence should really be kept throughout the day in all places. Each monastery is a house of prayer where sacred silence is fostered, nurtured, and maintained so that we might better hear the word of God at all times and more effectively and charitably speak that word to one another.

In the end, sacred silence only exists in order to hear God's words more effectively and to share that word with one another in love and in truth. It is never an end in itself. Jesus, the Word incarnate, is always the end and goal of all Christian monastic silence.

Our domestic members who live in their own homes throughout the world cannot experience monastic silence as completely as we do, even in an integrated monastery where celibates, singles, and families live together. Our domestic members must find specific times and places of silence to begin and/or end every day so that all activity and speech throughout each day is imbued with the spirit of silence that gives true meaning to every word and action.

We recommend spending twenty to thirty minutes each morning and evening in meditation that includes the discipline of silence. Many cannot do both morning and evening, so we encourage at least one period of twenty to thirty minutes daily. If they can only do one we recommend that they begin the day with an intentional time of silence. This helps set the tone of the rest of the day. If this is impractical, however, the evening is an acceptable time. What's important is that they spend at least twenty to thirty minutes in silence. Each day is spent in intentional silent prayer and meditation.

But the silent meditation periods in and of themselves are not enough. The real point of the silent meditation is the spirit of silence, reverent listening, and speech that is most charitable and effective. A good test for this is whether one feels compelled to comment on everything anyone says or whether one can remain silent and listen with interior contentment and peace. Only when one is a good listener can one be an effective speaker. So the discipline of silence carries over into the way we dialogue with everyone we encounter throughout our day.

There is an old axiom that remains true: "If you are afraid of silence then you cannot safely speak, and if you are afraid to speak then you cannot safely remain silent." So often filling in every silence with speech stems from a fear of silence. And remaining always silent often stems from a fear of stepping out in speech. In our silence and in our speech we must always be encountering the word of God without fear, with great trust, and with the great love that casts out all fear. This really is the goal of all monastic silence, both in ancient traditional monasticism and in the new monasticism being raised by the Spirit in the church today.

After decades of living in a community that embraces silence, I have kind of broken through to something wonderful. At first silence was difficult. It was rather wooden, repressive, and artificial. If you visited our community, you could tell that we were "working" at our silence. Today the older members observe silence in a genuine spirit of freedom and joy. It is life-giving and attractive to all. There is no shortcut to this state of silence. Each community and individual has to pass through these stages before silence becomes natural, easy, and life-giving. But I wholeheartedly believe that it has been well worth the journey. I invite you to begin the journey for yourself.

Stillness and Ministry

We live in a hyperactive civilization. We are constantly on the move. We rise early and go to bed late and move almost constantly the whole time we are awake. Consequently, we sleep poorly. The average household is a place of constant movement and noise. From the moment we wake we must get the household moving with the sound of children rising, getting ready for the day, preparing our breakfast, and then running off to work or getting the children to school. Since many parents work, both the mother and the father then run off to their respective careers in order to pay the bills of the constantly rising cost of raising a family in the West. Needless to say, this creates much stress within the average adult, not to mention the children of the typical Western family.

The monks of old had an answer to this dilemma. It's called "sacred stillness." In the Christian East, this has a Greek name: *Hesychia*. It gave rise to an entire movement in the fourteenth century called "the Hesychast movement." It was a monastic movement dedicated to rediscovering the call to solitude, silence, and stillness.

At the Hermitage we use an axiom that remains true: if you really want to do ministry well, then be content with stillness. It is only in the power of finding the Spirit in stillness that our ministry can really have the power of the Spirit in it at all. Plus, we recognize that behind every successful active ministry, there is usually a group of contemplative people praying in stillness for its success.

The same holds true for most of the monastic disciplines. If you are going to safely speak, then you must first enter into silence. If you want freedom, bind yourself under obedience to a spiritual leader and community. If you want the greatest wealth, embrace poverty. If you want the greatest communion, go into solitude and learn to live in chastity alone. The list of axioms go on and on, but they speak to a deeper paradoxical truth that rings true in every mindful human soul.

The Pond

Perhaps the greatest analogy for the sacred stillness is that of a pond. A Desert Father story goes like this: "They asked him to tell them how he himself had fared. He was silent for a while, and then poured water into a vessel and said, 'Look at the water,' and it was murky. After a little while he said again, 'See now, how clear the water has become.' As they looked into the water they saw their own faces, as in a mirror. Then he said to them, 'So it is with anyone who lives in the crowd; because of the turbulence, he does not see his sins: when he has been quiet, above all in solitude, then he recognizes his own faults.'"

The pond represents the human soul, person, and entire life. When the waters of the soul are agitated it does two things. First, it stirs up the sediment in the bottom of the pond so that the waters become unclear. Second, it causes the surface of the pond to become fractured and broken.

Likewise, when our life is hyperactive our soul is so stirred up that it becomes impossible to look into the deep waters to see what's really going on. We become so busy and muddled that it becomes most difficult to discern the movement of the Spirit of God within our soul. Things may originate with God, our own human power, or even the devil. But we cannot discern from which because our soul has become so muddy.

It's hard even to hear ourselves think, much less to discern the work of the Spirit of God or the work of darkness. God may be speaking clearly, but we cannot hear him above the cacophony of noise in our agitated life. He may be pointing the way, but we cannot see him because our view is obscured by the muddy waters of our soul. Consequently, our lives become confused, off course, and progressively less effective.

As to the second point, the human soul is created like a mirror to reflect the beautiful image of God. In the early days before mirrors, the average person looked into water to see his or her own reflection. When the surface of the pond of the soul is placid, it can reflect an undisturbed image. When the waters are agitated, the reflection is not completely impeded, but that reflection becomes fractured and broken. So, when we are hyperactive we lose the ability to reflect the beautiful image of God in an unbroken way.

The Spider

Another analogy that the monastic Hesychasts used was that of the spider. When a spider weaves its web, it sits perfectly still and waits for its prey to become caught in the web. It's able to discern when the prey has gotten caught in the web because the web moves. If the spider is agitated and moving, it cannot tell when the web is disturbed because the spider itself is moving the web. Only when the spider sits perfectly still can it discern any stirring of the web. Only then can the spider be nourished.

Likewise, when we take time for sacred stillness in our daily life we are able to discern any movement within our soul. Some of this movement is from the Spirit of God, and some of this movement is from darkness and can be a temptation. When we are still we can tell the difference, can choose the life-giving work of the Spirit, and can be nourished. If we are constantly moving we cannot really discern what's going on within our own soul, cannot tell the difference between the life-giving work of the Spirit of God or the things that rob us of life, and we therefore miss the wonderful nourishment of the Spirit that God gives us every day.

Mindful Watchfulness

Related to the gift of Hesychia, or sacred stillness, is what the Eastern fathers call "watchfulness." This is very similar to the modern concept of "mindfulness" that comes to us primarily from Buddhist teaching. Both simply mean becoming still enough that we can discern what's going on within our own life. Within the Christian tradition this would refer to every aspect of life: body, soul, spirit or senses, emotions, thoughts, and spiritual intuitions.

An example used by the Eastern monastic fathers for watchfulness is that of the serpent. This example has more to do with discerning and the work of darkness and temptation. They would say that if one is still and watchful, then one can discern when the serpent tries to enter the house of the soul as soon as the head of the serpent enters the door of the heart and mind. If one is too busy and not watchful, then one does not notice the serpent entering the house until the entire body is within. They would rightly contend that it's much easier to chop off the head of the serpent when only the head is within the door rather than waiting until the entire snake has entered the house of one's soul.

This is very similar to the teaching of St. Augustine in the West. He would teach that there are three states of temptation and sin and that it is much easier to conquer sin in the first stages. The first stage is the temptation itself. The stage is only on the level of thought and is only the suggestion to sin. No one is exempt from this stage. Even Jesus himself was tempted in every way we are, yet he was without sin. The second stage is also on the level of thought but moves to the emotions and senses as one toys with the temptation. The second stage constitutes a sin because one has made a choice to play with the temptation in one's thoughts. The third stage becomes more serious as thoughts stir up emotions and senses in action. This third stage is when internal sin reaches maturity and external sin.

He then goes on to say that it is easier to nip it in the bud than to let it grow into maturity. As we now say regarding sin, "Nip it in the bud." A good example of this would be in growing a tomato plant. Between two fruitful branches there will almost always be a sucker branch. It's very easy to reach down and to pinch off the sucker branch between one's thumb and fingers as long as you do it as soon as it appears. If you let it grow too long, then you must get a cutting implement to prune the plant. This is more difficult and more disturbing to the plant. Likewise, it's easier to stop the process of sin if you catch it early in the stage of mere temptation, or even in internal thought, rather than waiting until it stirs up the emotions and reaches fruition in action.

Meditation

On a practical daily level, Christian meditation is a great exercise in stillness. We begin by settling the body in a posture that is comfortable but attentive. We recommend simply sitting straight in a straight-back chair, neither too soft, like a lounge chair, nor too hard, like a straight-backed wooden chair. The main point is to give the body something to do that is minimal so that it will not fidget and squirm during the twenty- to thirty-minute meditation. Next we still the breath by slowing it down and breathing deeply. Again, we give it something to do but not something that will distract us. Once the body and breath are still, the mind begins to slow down so that it can more easily focus. Once the mind slows down and focuses, the emotions soon follow. Soon, the body and breath, the mind and emotions settle down and become still.

The point of this stillness is to better discern the action of God in our life. Stillness is never itself the goal. God remains the goal. Jesus remains the way. Once we learn the way of Hesychia we soon discover the way of Jesus, who was active in ministry and mission even when he was in prayerful and sacred stillness.

It is said of St. Francis that he sought "not so much to pray but to become a prayer." The story is also told that once he took a brother into town to preach. They spent most of the day walking among the merchants and townspeople, greeting everyone with love and joy and conversing with them about how business was going and how their families were doing. After a few hours St. Francis said to the brother, "Let's go home." The brother was shocked. He expected to go out and preach with the great St. Francis. So he said, "I thought we were going to preach." St. Francis responded, "We've been preaching all day." Often we do the greatest preaching by simply learning how to be with God and how to be with others. Sacred stillness teaches us this gift through the stillness and activity of each day.

I'm also reminded of the lesson of St. Francis where he says that it is not the preachers who will be rewarded by God for converting the masses but the contemplative brothers in the far-off and isolated hermitages scattered throughout the mountains and hills. Often it is our sacred stillness that brings the greatest missionary activity. And if active ministry does not first flow from contentment in sacred stillness, then that ministry runs the risk of being self-serving. Ministry that bears the fruit of the Spirit must begin by nurturing a life in the Spirit by taking times of sacred stillness and allowing a sacred stillness to permeate every activity of our life. Good active ministry flows from sacred stillness, and good active ministry leads others back into sacred stillness.

All of these are examples of how and why sacred stillness is an important part of everyone's daily life. It is essential to the universal monk. The new monasticism is a modern spiritual movement where we emphasize the profound importance of the ancient practice of Hesychia, or sacred stillness. We also give some specific teachings on how to make this inactivity part of one's daily life. Let's move on now to the related ideas of solitude and silence and times and places to make these active in our life.

Integration

We live in a world of warring factions and divisions. There are divisions in ideology and politics. There are divisions between nations. Gangs battle one another for control of turf and for people on the streets of the world's cities. There are divisions between religions, especially as fundamentalism grows throughout the religions of the world. This even causes divisions within the church. There are divisions between and within Christian churches. As the gap between liberals and ultra-conservatives widens, the battle intensifies. Our daily lives are fractured because time is torn between a million things that meet our ever-growing needs and wants and those of our families. Then there are divisions within our own human makeup. We often find ourselves fractured emotionally, intellectually, and spiritually. We are divided and fractured on every level. The answer is a fully integrated life.

One of the greatest expressions of the new monastic communities is integration. Integration takes seeming opposites and unites them into a living whole. This is a practical expression of the mystery of paradox. Paradox is the greatest gateway to the mysterious aspect of the Being we call "God." The new monasticism integrates spiritualities and states of life that have sometimes seemed opposed to one another in the past.

Jesus symbolizes it on the cross for Christians. Through outstretched arms, thorn-crowned head, and nailed hands and feet, he reaches to unite and harmonize the left and the right, the high and the low, in his sacred body. Each dies to its own limited and self-serving needs in order to be fully integrated into a larger whole that preserves the integrity of them all. It more than satisfies each one's needs.

In the documents and teachings for the Brothers and Sisters of Charity, we say that integration is not the same as musical synthesis. In music, synthesis distorts a sound to unite it with another sound to make it appear to sound like something that it is not. This can be heard in synthesized "strings," where the sound of an orchestra is approximated. Integration does not try to appear as something it is not. It is completely itself. Each sound is retained in purity but can join with others to create a beautiful harmony bigger than just one note or sound.

The early church writings, or patristics, often used the analogy of music to describe this integration. They would say that it is like the strings of a harp. Each string is tuned to make a beautiful harmony with the others. Each string retains its individual note, but the listener hears a larger harmonious sound. The same is said of a choir. Each singer must fully and sensitively sing his or her own note, but he or she joins together with others singing their own notes as well in order to make a bigger and more beautiful sound.

We say that our integration is like the strands of a rope. It is like a Franciscan cord. Each strand combines with the other in order to make something stronger than itself. But each is still visible when you look at the rope. The more strands that are integrated, the stronger the rope. So we try to integrate as much of the work of God into our community life as we can while not distorting the integrity of any strand.

This integration can also be seen as praying hands. Many of these integrations are like two hands. At times in our experience they can seem to be at odds with one another, perhaps even clenching fists that collide, or are often used for violence. But in the fully integrated body they can first join together, relax, and intertwine or join individual fingers and become praying hands. Then they can coordinate together in one body as they do the work of the body. They can become instruments of peace.

Let's briefly take a look at some of these integrations.

The most ancient integration is between solitude and community. St. Antony of the Desert did not found a community. It was more a colony of hermits. St. Pachomius founded an organized community that had formal leadership and living arrangements and common times for prayer, meals, and work. Antony's hermit colonies lived in solitude during the week and gathered weekly for fellowship and Mass. Pachomius's community was together every day. In history both the East and the West have tried to integrate these two streams in various ways. In the East the monasteries and sketes of Mount Athos and in the West the monasteries with hermitages like the Camaldolese, Carthusians, and many others represent this.

Today, the new monasticism also tries to do this. Most new communities have hermitages as well as common buildings, including a chapel, kitchen, dining room, and work areas. Some just emphasize the solitude of one's cell or room within a community house. Some of these are in urban areas, and some are more expanded in rural areas. Some have additional time during the week or month for greater solitude.

At Little Portion Hermitage this amounts to a classical pattern of hermitages scattered according to state of life around a large monastery that includes a chapel and all other common areas. Our domestic members who live in their own homes find a helpful pattern from the colonies of St. Antony of the Desert. They find daily solitude in their prayer corners or rooms in their houses, and they come together weekly for their respective parish church worship and weekly, bimonthly, or monthly in their cell groups for mutual support in living this life in today's world.

We are also what the Catholic Church calls a "mixed" community made up of celibate men and women. Each sex has its own segregated and private area: a brothers' grove patterned after the simple hermitages of St. Francis and a sisters' skete patterned after the more common arrangement of the Carthusians who have a common cloister connecting the individual hermit cells and gardens.

Many question the sexual temptations in this arrangement, but our experience is that this happens no more frequently than in more segregated communities. If someone wants a romantic relationship, he or she will always find a way to engage in it, regardless of segregated living areas.

We also integrate celibates and families. Families live in their own private area that meets their unique needs. Their cells are very simple by our cultural standards but considerably larger than the celibate cells, with a small kitchen and dining room and living rooms and bedrooms for couples and families with children. They also have a playground far enough away so as not to create too much noise throughout the rest of the monastery. Couples without children tend to live in another area so each person can experience greater solitude and silence.

This mixed life with celibate men and women and the integration of families seems to be a rather widespread characteristic of the new monasticism, though it is not universal to all new communities.

Another integration has to do with prayer styles. We integrate the charismatic and the contemplative. This can be tricky. Sometimes they come off more like opposed fists than praying hands! But you really need both hands to have a fully balanced prayer life. In times past, these two groups have often lapsed into a rather skeptical view of each other. Charismatics sometimes think that contemplatives are too "New Age" and theologically liberal, and contemplatives sometimes think that charismatics are too emotional and theologically conservative. This is unfortunate but true.

We like to see these two expressions like breathing. There are two motions, in and out. Without either, we die. Breathing in is like being filled with the wonderful positive things of God, Jesus, the church, and all the gifts of the Spirit. Breathing out is like the contemplative action of letting go of absolutely everything—possessions, relationships, and even our very self—so that God can use everything according to his plans rather than our own. One is enthusiastic, the other quiet. While each person naturally tends one way or the other, the well-balanced spiritual life needs a bit of both.

Related to this is the integration of the liturgical and the spontaneous. As a monastic community, we pray the Divine Office with a Communion Service or Mass daily. As a charismatic and contemplative community, we use the form of liturgical prayer but leave ample time for silence and spontaneous prayer throughout. We often leave room for charismatic gifts after the readings or Communion and sing enthusiastically in the Spirit throughout the Mass. We also leave time for contemplative silence after each psalm and again after Communion or charismatic gifts. A natural balance seems to result. At times we may go through seasons of more contemplative or charismatic times in the prayer of the community, but the structure itself leaves time for both. We also sing the psalms rather than merely recite them. These tend to make the experience more prayerful and charismatic within the liturgical form itself. As Augustine said, "Those who sing, pray twice!" The two can actually become one once the two are given a chance to fully operate.

We also integrate faith expressions. We are a Roman Catholic community, but we have many non-Catholics who find great strength by joining us. We find creative ways to include them in the day in and day out life of the community.

We integrate all religions from a Christian base, all Christian faiths from our Catholic base, and all religious and monastic traditions from a Franciscan base. Nevertheless, we are not a formal Franciscan community but are unique and new. Franciscanism is our mother, but we are a child that is unique and new. We will always love our mother, but we cannot go back into the womb.

We also integrate a contemplative base and ministries that go out into the world. This integrates the classical Benedictine stability with Franciscan itinerancy. It also draws inspiration from the wandering sannyasi of Hindus and the bodhisattvas of Buddhism. It can be hard to pull off. When ministers go out, it leaves a real gap in the local monastery. But when we never go out, we can easily stagnate.

For our domestics this means maintaining a stable home life and job and reaching out in appropriate forms of ministry. This is found in the establishment of our cell groups, parish ministry, and work with the poor in their local areas. In today's busy lifestyle, we encourage folks to spend quality time with their families and to participate in a weekly cell group, another time for parish activity, and Sunday and holy day Mass or worship.

Each of these integrations really deserves a complete treatment. But for us these integrations developed very simply out of the life we lived and the folks we attracted. We never started out to be novel. It just evolved. After that we had to figure out what it all meant, where it fit in monastic and Franciscan history, and how it worked out in church law. But all those things happened under the inspiration of the Holy Spirit and the kind and wise guidance of some great Franciscans and monks that God brought into our path to help us discern these things.

Integration remains probably one of the most distinguishing aspects of the universal new monasticism. It builds on the old but becomes something that has never been seen before.

It is like a rock wall. Each stone must be placed squarely on top of the ones that have come before. But it must go into a place where no stone has ever been before. Placing the stone of our life and community firmly on what has come before is conservative. Going into a new space is progressive. If you try to go into a higher new space without building on what has come before, you fall to the ground and crack. If you simply try to repeat what has come before, you cannot go higher and cannot really displace the old. You must do both to be fully alive in the church and in Christ. That is part of the witness of these new monastic communities.

But there is an even deeper integration that applies to all of us. It is the integration of our very self within us. St. Paul says that we are created whole and entire, spirit, soul, and body (1 Thess 5:23). The problem is that we have gotten turned upside down and fractured ourselves into pieces.

Most of us function on the level of the body and the soul and have forgotten the spirit altogether. The body includes the five senses and the physical part of emotions and thoughts. The soul includes the spiritual mind beyond mere brain activity, or the reasonable self inside. When we begin to function there primarily and exclusively, we tend to judge our life according to our sensual or emotional comfort levels. When they are threatened, we become unhappy. Senses, emotions, and thoughts are not bad. But they are not the whole story of the human being.

There is a deeper self or being that God created to be primary. It is the spirit. Our spirit is deeper than senses, emotions, or thoughts. It is pure intuition. It is beyond the limitations of sensual pleasures, emotional ups or downs, or intellectual ideas and opinions. It is beyond space and time. All these things come and go. They change and develop. Only the spirit remains constant and the same. It is stable in a very unstable world.

This does not mean fracturing or denying who we really are. Quite the opposite. We deny our old self so that we might discover who we really are in God. The old self is fractured. The senses, emotions, and thoughts have become clouded and unhealthy, so the spirit is lost or sleeping. This means we are internally incomplete and divided. So we are usually unhappy deep down inside. We carry around our old sensual, emotional, and thought patterns. They do not make us happy, but often we are afraid to let them go. When we dare to really let go of the old patterns completely, we are born again in the original image and pattern of God within our human being. As spirit is rediscovered, the senses, emotions, and thoughts are reborn and reintegrated in their proper place. The spirit was never gone. It was deep inside but covered with the old and false self. When we really let go of that old person, that false self, then we are free to be born again to the person God originally made us to be.

That self is fully integrated. Once the intuitive self of the spirit is rediscovered, every other faculty is born again as well. Thoughts begin to facilitate the primary life of the spirit. Emotions empower that life, and the sensual self of the body houses it. Every faculty finds its right place and functions fully without hindrance. Like a train that has had its wheels set back on track, we can now travel smoothly the course of our human life to God. We have been reintegrated.

The Trinity is our greatest example of integration. There is one God and three Persons. You cannot know one without knowing the other, but they are three distinct persons. If you know the Father, you also know the other two. Likewise with the Son and the Spirit. Like the Trinity, our body, soul, and spirit become reintegrated and united, with each doing its own part in the oneness of our human being.

Jesus and the new monasticism give us ways to let go of the old self that is trapped in illusion and desire (Col 3:1-3).

It is an entire way of life that helps us to really let go of the old self and be born again as the person God originally created us to be. Meditation and prayer are primary ways to do this. But community is where it is supported and tested. The entire lifestyle is geared toward this wonderful end. Everything in our life becomes a prayer. We become a walking meditation.

I remember a story that a Cistercian monk, Fr. Basil Pennington, once told me. He was talking with a Buddhist monk about the practice of meditation. The Buddhist asked Basil what his particular practice was. Basil gestured around the entire monastery and said, "This is my practice." The Buddhist understood at once and smiled.

The Cross
Spirit, Soul, and Body

"Gal. 6:14-15—The Rule (of the brothers and sisters) is the cross of our Lord Jesus Christ.

We should be troubled about nothing except this all-encompassing rule.

All that matters is that one be created anew." (Scripture Rule, The Brothers and Sisters of Charity, Chapter 1)

The Rule of the Cross

The Scripture Rule of the Brothers and Sisters of Charity begins with the above reference to St. Paul's letter to the Galatians. It says that the cross and resurrection of our Lord Jesus Christ are the all-encompassing rule of our entire way of life. It is the basis for all sacraments, beginning with baptism, and the profession of our monastic commitment. Dying to the old self and arising a new person in Christ is the basis for the entire rest of our way of life. You cannot live our life without reaching this beginning place, and you can never go beyond it without losing the reason for our entire way of life. It is the beginning and the end and the center of all we are about.

Why?

Spirit, Soul, and Body

Scripture tells us what we are made of and who we really are. It says that we are "whole and entire, spirit, soul, and body" (1 Thess 5:23). We are an integrated whole, but each part has meaning and purpose. Most of us think of ourselves as "body, soul, and spirit." And in reality most of us think only of body and soul. The church in the West has taught that we are body and soul, but most of the great theologians separate a lower and higher soul. There is a real confusion about the difference between soul and spirit. But Hebrews 4 says that the word of God is sharper than a two-edged sword and can penetrate between "soul and spirit." What do body, soul, and spirit really mean?

The body is our senses. This includes the five basic senses of touch, sight, hearing, taste, and smell. But it also includes the physical stuff of emotions and brain thought. It has been proven that much of our emotions are chemical, and our brain functions through electricity and chemistry. When these things are imbalanced, it effects our emotions and thoughts. Imbalance in the basic five senses also creates imbalance and ill health. But as important as these things are, they are only the external part of the human being.

The soul moves to the spiritual mind. It is cognition. Many medieval manuscripts use "soul" and "mind" interchangeably. St. Bonaventure's great work, the *Itinerarium*, is sometimes translated "The Journey of the Soul to God" and sometimes "The Journey of the Mind to God." So the "soul" includes thoughts but in a more spiritual sense than mere brain thought. While this gets to the interior part of our being, it is still not the deepest aspect of who we are.

The spirit is where we get to the very essence of who we are, and it is the most overlooked human faculty. The spirit is beyond senses, emotions, or thoughts. It is pure spiritual intuition. It is the part of us that simply "knows" reality. It is the part of us that enters into pure contemplation beyond images, names, or forms into a pure union with the One Who Is. It is similar to, but deeper than, conscience, which uses the objective part of the mind as well as the spirit, and must be formed through proper teaching and guidance. The fathers teach us that even the human spirit has the capacity for the infinite in the Spirit of God; can be in the past, present, and future all at once; and can "know" all things on the level of intuition but not on the level of rational thought (only God knows all things in this omniscient way). When you consider that our perception of even the natural world is most limited in comparison to the eleven to sixteen alternate dimensions of time and space as described in modern physics, or the string theory of everything regarding the harmony of all physical things, such a knowledge of the spirit inspires us to its expansive personal potential.

In original creation, the spirit was first in our understanding of who we are. It was facilitated by the soul and housed in the body. Spiritual intuition beyond time, space, and objective senses, emotions, or forms was our primary mode of existence. We walked with an entirely expanded spiritual sense of being and knowing. This was facilitated by thought, empowered by the enthusiasm of emotion, and housed in the physical body of the senses. We functioned in a radically different way than we do now.

Through sin we have turned this wonder of our being upside down and almost entirely forgotten the faculty of the spirit. Most of us call our day "good" or "bad" based on how our body is doing. It might also include how well our business or personal relationships are going. These things are real and important, but they do not constitute our deepest well-being. They are discerned first through the awareness of thought, and it affects our emotions, which in turn affects our body again.

The spirit gets almost entirely forgotten. So we function in an incomplete way. In one sense we are really only functioning as partly human because we are leaving out the most basic faculty of our human being: the spirit!

The Old Self

The cross is the way to get things turned round right again. We have to bring our disordered self to the cross and let it go completely. We have to "let it die." St. Paul calls this dying to the "old self" (Eph 4). Jesus repeatedly calls us to take up our cross to follow him and says that unless we die to our self we cannot really be his follower and find out who we truly are.

When we die to the old self we let go of our upside-down misidentity. Most of us walk around with a false identity! Think about it. Most of us think of ourselves as someone we really are not. We think of ourselves as a self we have allowed ourselves to become, a self that is only partially true, only partially "us" as God originally created us.

When we hold on to the old self we get proverbial "ego attachments." This means that we attach our identity to false images of ourselves. These are found in confusing our essential self with our external senses, emotions, or thoughts. We have senses, emotions, and thoughts, but our essential self is much deeper than these things. The problem arises when these things are challenged or inconvenienced. When we do not get the sensual gratifications we want, we get upset. Likewise, when we do not get "fame or fortune," the affirmation, acknowledgement, or control that we want, we get upset. The reason we get upset is that we have attached our identity to these real but nonetheless external aspects of our life.

When we let go of this self-identity, this old self, these things may come and go, but we remain at peace. It has not affected our essential being. When we have the courage to really let go of the self that we think we are, we find out who we really are!

Energies and Essence

According to the Eastern Christian fathers, there is a difference between energies and essence. Though this cannot be stated absolutely, we can summarize that energies are the outer part of anything that can be perceived through the faculties of body and soul: senses, emotions, or thoughts. Essence is the deepest being of anything. It can only be perceived through the intuitive faculty of the spirit. This takes on a special significance with humanity and with God. Our body and soul are human energies because they can be perceived through senses, emotions, or thoughts in the world of phenomenon. Our spirit is our essence because it can only be perceived through the intuitive faculty. As Scripture says, "Among human beings, who knows what pertains to a person except the spirit of the person that is within? Similarly, no one knows what pertains to God except the Spirit of God" (1 Cor 2:11). God's energies are called "uncreated energies" and pertain to things that can be known about God. God's essence is beyond all perceptions of senses, emotions, or thoughts and can only be perceived through the intuitions of the Spirit in our spirit. Energies can be known through meditation on Scripture and devotion. Essence can only be known through contemplation beyond all senses, emotions, or thoughts. It is Spirit to spirit and Essence to essence. Once found, then we see the essence at work in every energy of God, humanity, and creation.

The way that we do this is through the classical practice of sacred reading, vocal prayer, meditation, and contemplation within the context of a monastic community under a rule and the spiritual direction of an abbot. Then we can effectively reach out to the entire world with the love of God that is not self-obsessed and is in the right order of God and the Spirit. This is the greatest gift we have to give to the world, and it cannot be given until it is received. The new monasticism helps us receive this gift.

Meditation

Meditation is a very popular practice and topic nowadays. We see articles on it in health and wellness magazines in doctors' offices all the time. We hear of Christian meditation as well as Eastern meditation. Folks are hungry for it and are seeking out resources to help them engage in it in their personal lives. The way of the universal monk makes this practice available to everyone and provides a daily means to grow in it.

There is a clear connection between meditation and health. Doctors are now telling us that meditation brings relaxation and peace and assists the process of healing as well as the prevention of disease. Some have noticed that meditation releases endorphins into the body and brain that bring peace and that parts of the brain are stimulated in healing ways during meditation.

Some researchers studying the new physics of string theory tell us that the basic stuff of the universe is strings that vibrate at different speeds. These vibrating strings make a certain "music" when everything is in harmony. When things are discordant, there is conflict and agitation. Meditation brings us back into harmony on every level where once there may have been discord.

There has been a real cross-pollination between the world religions regarding meditation in recent years. Most of this is due to the sheer availability of source materials with modern publishing and the internet. There is a veritable knowledge resource revolution going on in our lifetime, and the world has become a true global village regarding access to knowledge.

Some regard religious cross-pollination most healthy and strengthening. Others see it as a pollution of the purity of the authentic message of any specific religion. Christianity is no exception. Both positions hold some truth. I believe that as long as we are strong in our base faith first, then an expansion into another's faith will only enrich our own. But if we are not first grounded and strong in our own faith, we can often end up confused and can lose the little faith we thought we had, ending up with nothing. This is not an idle caution.

But what does "meditation" mean? The West and the East often mean two opposite things by their use of the words "meditation" and "contemplation." For the West, meditation precedes contemplation and includes a focusing of the mind and directing of the heart after the disciplining of the body. For the East, contemplation means what we in the West call meditation. In the East, they use meditation to mean the passing over beyond senses, emotions, or thoughts into the unconditioned state of pure being with Being often called "Samadhi." We call a similar state "contemplation."

But for the average person, meditation simply means the stilling and focusing of the body, mind, and emotions to find inner peace and awakening. From that peace comes more clarity of thought, healthier emotional enthusiasm, and more effective action that really accomplishes good in our daily life. We calm body, mind, and emotions to break through to something more essentially real but beyond external senses, emotions, or conceptual thoughts. When we break through to this Reality, then Reality permeates all that we are and makes daily life more real and more effective. Thoughts are clarified, emotions are purified, and the body becomes the vehicle for a better life in this world.

For the Christian that Reality is God. The unique way of the Christian is through the way, truth, and life of Jesus Christ. Jesus is the historical man in space and time. Christ is his presence through all the cosmos for all eternity. Jesus Christ shows us the way to God, who is as intimate and loving as a good father, so Jesus called him "Father." He shows us a way to God, who is Pure Spirit, who he called the "Holy Spirit." Other teachers from other religions also teach wonderful ways to meditate. Jesus shows us a way, truth, and life that make his entire life a complete meditation that compliments all for his followers and for anyone who chooses to follow his way. This is found in his incarnation where divinity takes on humanity to restore humanity to divinity through everything in his life. But this is found most especially in his complete *kenosis*, or "self emptying," on the cross. It is the Paradox of paradoxes and shows us the great goal of all the meditation teachers. In meditation we learn how to find ourselves by losing ourselves. This reality is most powerful in Jesus Christ.

In Christian tradition there are many ways of meditation. Most of these involve focusing the mind on certain realities of the faith based on the teaching and life of Jesus. These are often experienced according to spiritual schools such as Benedictine, Cistercian, Franciscan, Dominican, Carmelite, Jesuit, and so on. Each school has its own gift and often its own method of meditation. Briefly, but not exhaustively stated, Benedictines focus on the method of sacred reading, or *lectio*. Cistercians often focus on charity and love, especially through the love song of Scripture, the Song of Songs. Franciscans focus on the goodness and love of God found most fully in the life and poverty of Christ. Dominicans use prayerful study of God's word in Scripture and apostolic tradition. Carmelites focus on the Spiritual Espousal. Jesuits use a most intense mental and emotional method of stages and progressions to God. In the Christian East the use of the

Jesus Prayer under the guidance of a spiritual father is most powerful. Protestants focus more on Scripture alone but are recently showing great interest for some of the other schools of meditation as well.

Seated Meditation

Most people today are interested in what we would call "seated meditation." Though the term comes from the East, most folks are not interested in much but what works for them on a daily basis. For most of us it simply makes sense to sit down comfortably so that we can meditate and pray for a longer period of time. We are not really interested in some kind of esoteric posture from the Far East.

In the West most folks are most comfortable in a straight-back chair. Some like to sit on the floor. It is a good posture for staying grounded and connected to reality. We remember that "humility" means being "brought low to the earth." A cross-legged position is good for most. But it is important that we not get stiff or cut off circulation to the legs and such.

Posture

This brings out the importance of posture in meditation. In seated meditation we want to give the body something minimal to do so that we will not have to be continually distracted by the body.

Sitting is best done in a straight-back chair with feet flat on the floor. We sit straight but comfortable. There should be nothing militarily rigid about it. But we should not lounge or slouch. Slouching will cut off circulation to various parts of the body and cause aches and pains. This will create the need to move and shift. We want to stay as still as possible. Each time we move, we have to process it with thought. We want to focus our thoughts on the meditation.

Good posture restores the health and comfort that make meditation possible without distraction. In order to get a good curve in the small of the back, I recommend pushing the small of the back against the back of the chair. Once this is done you will probably find that you do not really need to sit back against the back of the chair with your shoulders or upper back. It is a very natural way to sit, kind of like sitting on a horse. You can ride with comfort and flexibility.

Some folks tend to let their heads fall back or off to one side or the other. This often gives rise to neck pain. I recommend that we imagine a string extending from the crown of the head and pulling that string until our head straightens out naturally. The nose should then align with the navel and the ears with the shoulders.

These rather physical disciplines of posture should be used only if you do not have any back or neck problems that would make them impossible or hurtful. Use common sense. At the same time, sometimes we have grown so accustomed to unhealthy postures that when we try to correct them it feels uncomfortable at first. If this is the case, hang in there with the newer and healthier posture. It will cause you to feel better in the long run.

I recommend that you rest your hands on your lap with the palms open. The Franciscans were part of a movement in the thirteenth century called the mendicants. "Mendicant" means "open handed." It was used for those who were completely empty and poor and relied on God and his people to fill them. Today this is a good posture for meditation. It causes us, in a posture of openness and trust, to let go of anything we are clinging to. It physically prepares us to spiritually rest completely in God.

People invariably close their eyes in meditation. This is sometimes good, but it can also be bad. Quite often in today's busy lifestyle, when we close our eyes we tend to drift off to sleep. We might need more sleep, but this is not the real goal of meditation! We want to rest but focus. Nevertheless, if we keep our eyes wide open, we tend to start looking around at this or that, and again we are distracted. So I recommend keeping the eyes neither fully open nor shut but comfortably lowered. Some people like to focus on a candle, crucifix, or icon. But whatever we use, we do not want to begin "looking" at it and mentally fantasizing or drifting. I tell people to imagine a line of infinity at about a forty-five-degree angle down that symbolizes God's infinity. This will give their eyes something to do so that we will stay awake but without wandering eyes.

Folks sometimes object to using these postures and want to just sit like they are used to. I would ask you to give them a try before you reach that conclusion. These postures really do symbolize all the physical disciplines of asceticism that, when rightly used, prepare the way for a better and less distracted spiritual life. As with all healthy asceticism or discipline, the deeply ingrained bad habits often cry out in every protest imaginable to try to get us to give up and retreat into the old comfortable habits that might be killing us. But we must keep going if we are to win the victory.

Breath

One of the great physical tools to use to help rest and focus is breath. It is found almost universally in the developed meditation methods of the great religions of the world. Christianity is no exception.

Some more conservative Christians are afraid of this because of teachings they have heard that demons are united with this form. In some cases they are right. But the breath has been united with Christian tradition for over fifteen hundred years. If used in the right way, it can be most beneficial to our Christian meditation.

The word used for "Spirit" in both the Hebrew and Christian Scriptures means "air," "wind," and "breath." In Hebrew it is *Ruach*, and in Greek it is *Pneuma*. It is the root of what we call "pneumatic," or "air powered," tools. It is also why we sometimes call breathing "respiration," or "re-spiriting."

The early church wanted to follow St. Paul's injunction to "pray without ceasing." At first they prayed the Lord's Prayer three times a day: morning, noon, and night. They also came together on the day of Jesus' resurrection, Sunday, or the first day of the Hebrew week, to celebrate the Eucharist, hear God's word, and experience fellowship together. But they wanted something more. What could they do? What tool could they use to help pray without ceasing?

So what do we do without ceasing? We breathe. I have seen people born, and I have seen them die. It is the first and the last thing we all do. We breathe when we are happy or sad, awake or asleep. If we are still alive we had better be breathing!

In the fifth century there was a bishop named Diodochus from Macedonia in a little town called Photice, or Photiki. He taught the people of Photice to unite the name and person of Jesus Christ to every breath they breathed. The Jesus Prayer was born. But it was still in its infancy. This developed in time through the trials and errors of experience. Sometimes they prayed only one part or even one word of the prayer. Sometimes they just repeated, "Jesus." Eventually, it became set into a formula that is taught with great sophistication by the monks of the Christian East, especially on Mount Athos. We will look into the Jesus Prayer in greater detail elsewhere.

Today, people use the same tool of breath prayer in different ways to bring out certain aspects of their life with and in Jesus Christ.

The first thing to do is simply to breathe deeply. We breathe from the diaphragm, like we do when we sing. The way you can test if you are doing this or not is to see if your stomach expands when you breathe in. Imagine a little line from your nostrils to just below your navel that air follows as you breathe in and out through the nose.

Most adults have developed an unfortunate habit of breathing from their upper chests during waking hours. This means we are only using about one third of our lungs and only a small part of the blood is being oxygenated. This makes us feel sluggish and tired. But children breathe from their bellies. We do too when we are deeply relaxed or when we sleep. Learning to breathe "from our bellies" helps us breathe deeply.

Breathing should be gentle, not forced. There are some techniques that use hard breathing that you can hear. Others say that the breath should become so gentle that it will not even move a feather that is placed before the nostrils. For our purposes I recommend breathing gently so that when you really get the hang of it, it is almost beyond hearing. I recommend starting with a slow cleansing breath to the count of a slow ten on the in breath and six or seven or so on the out breath. After this we can return to a more natural but still slower rhythm of breathing.

A Way

In Itinerant Ministry I lead meditation through a song simply called "Breathe." In it we take a little journey. After very briefly teaching the people how to sit and breathe as we just mentioned, the first verse simply asks us to breathe in the Spirit of God. The in breath is a filling breath with all that is good and wonderful from the Spirit of God. We do not get too intellectual or specific. We simply intuit these wonderful realities in our life. As we breathe out, we simply let go of anything in our life that is standing between us and the things of God. Again, this is not something intellectual. It is intuited. We simply let go.

The things in our life that are not of God eventually bring us pain and suffering. If we do not change but remain in that place, we begin to share that pain and suffering with everyone we touch. Jesus comes to heal us of that pain by taking it on the cross and resurrecting to confirm that it is gone forever for those who follow his way, truth, and life.

The second verse is about Jesus. Here, we breathe in the name and person of Jesus and everything good, beautiful, and true about Jesus. As we breathe out, we simply let go of anything that is keeping us from being like Jesus in our own daily life. We let go of sin and pride.

In the chorus we breathe in the deepest essence of God and let go of anything external that keeps us from breaking through to that essence through contemplation. We pass through the dying and rising of Jesus on the cross as we bring the old self to the foot of the cross and just let it go. Then, the original person God created us to be when we were created in our mother's womb can be awakened and born again in the Spirit of God through Jesus.

We conclude by breathing in the healing of God that comes when we really let go and let God. We learn how to breathe in this healing with every breath we breathe. This is the breath of the Spirit. It is the Spirit of Jesus.

I also teach how to walk through the senses, thoughts, and emotions, realizing them and letting them go through the cross of Jesus in order to find the spirit resurrected through the Spirit of Jesus. Here you just focus on each faculty, acknowledge how each is doing today, realize that they easily change and are conditioned by things that happen to us in the changing world. So we bring them to the cross and completely let them go. By letting them go, we are able to break through to the spirit beyond senses, emotions, or thoughts. Then, the spirit permeates and renews them all so that the thoughts facilitate the spirit, the emotions become enthusiastic (or "in theos" or "in God") again, and the senses of the body become the vehicle for this wonderful spiritual reality to function in the material and phenomenal world.

There are many ways and methods of using the breath in Christian meditation. These are just a couple that I teach in retreat and Itinerant Ministry. They have all been met with great success.

Time and Space

Before we leave off, it is good to mention again that we need to set aside a time and space for meditation. If you do not do this, I can promise you that most folks will simply not get it done. I recommend a prayer corner or room in your cell or house devoted exclusively to this end. Put some prayer aids in it, like a cross, crucifix, candle, or icon, but keep it free from clutter, especially secular clutter like magazines, laptops, and such.

The next thing is time. It usually takes about twenty minutes to enter into good meditation. Out of that twenty, you will probably get about two minutes of real contemplation. And that will be enough to last the rest of the day. Do not let any excuse keep you from this time of contemplation. It is one of the most important things you do all day.

Lectio Divina

Related to meditation is the classical monastic practice of *lectio divina*, or "sacred reading." This is a slow, prayerful reading of sacred texts that is distinct from theological study. Its main purpose is to lead to prayer and union with God.

The Rule of St. Benedict mentions *lectio divina*. In chapter 48 on manual labor it says, "Idleness is the enemy of the soul. Therefore, the brothers [and sisters] should have specified periods for manual labor as well as for prayerful reading" (RB 48.1). It goes on to arrange for nearly two hours of *lectio divina* during ordinary days and three hours during Lent.

That the teaching on *lectio* in the Rule of St. Benedict is found in the chapter on manual labor is significant. It means that prayer does not exclude work, and work cannot be properly done without prayer. Work without prayer becomes dry and lifeless. Prayer without work becomes self-serving and idle.

Originally, *lectio divina* was simply a phrase to describe prayerful reading of Scripture. Origen was the first to use it. It was not the more fully developed use that we have today. It simply meant to ponder prayerfully the word of God during study. He did not have a separate understanding of theological study and *lectio*. Today the Orthodox similarly do not separate dogmatic and mystical theology as we have done in the West. For them, one must be a mystic to be a theologian. I tend to agree.

In later generations, a full program of *lectio* developed in the West that also included prayer, meditation, and contemplation. It was a fourfold progression of *lectio, oratio, meditatio*, and *contemplatio*, or sacred reading, prayer, meditation, and contemplation. Today when we say *lectio*, this fourfold progression is usually implied. Let's take a quick look at what these mean.

Lectio

We have already described some of *lectio divina*. It is a prayerful pondering of the sacred text. The text itself is usually Scripture but can also include the writings of the saints and mystics, especially from the monastic tradition. The West tends to emphasize Scripture before patristic and monastic writers. The East tends to emphasize reading patristics in order to properly understand the Scriptures. Either way, it is not a theological study of going through endless cross-references and word studies. But even these things can be considered *lectio* in the broad sense if done in a slower, prayerful way. The point of *lectio* is prayer, not intellectual knowledge alone.

Oratio

This simply means prayer. Specifically it means vocal prayer, or the prayers that are said out loud either in public prayer or in private. For the ancients, when one prayed or meditated, they actually said the prayers out loud or at least silently formed the words with their lips.

Why? Because it slows us down. Today we are often trained to speed-read texts. This gets us through great volumes of material and even lets us retain what they mean. But we cannot get the deeper spiritual meaning of a text when it is read quickly.

My wife was trained in the older ways of a monastic community when she was younger. She was taught that when she prayed the Divine Office in private or prayed devotional prayers, she was to form the words with her lips as she read. I have noticed the same thing with older monks and friars that guided me on my spiritual journey. They say that they were trained to form the words with their lips specifically to get them to slow down when they read and to really ponder the words. It also aided in memorization.

But prayer is not just an external exercise of reading words out loud. This can be an abuse at the other extreme from speed-reading. Far too often folks "say their prayers" without really going deeper into the spiritual things of the heart and mind. Real prayer allows the text to soak into the deeper recesses of the heart and mind, the soul and spirit. It uses words but stirs emotions and senses and opens the way to the places of the spirit beyond all words. Here we can be reminded that Mary pondered these things in her heart (see Luke 2:19). We must do the same if we are to really pray.

Meditatio

Again, due to the rise of the practice of Eastern meditation, there is some confusion between meditation and contemplation in the Christian world. In the East, "meditation" comes from the word *samadhi*, which means complete absorption. When Easterners speak of "contemplation," they mean to mentally contemplate certain truths. Christian tradition uses the words in exactly the opposite way. We use "meditation" to mean to focus the mind on particular aspects of the faith. For us, "contemplation" means passing beyond ideas, thoughts, and forms. In other words, when we say "meditate" we mean what Hindus, Buddhists, and even Taoists mean by "contemplate." When we say "contemplation," we mean what they mean by the word "meditation" or *samadhi*. But the word "meditate" has a history of its own in the Middle East.

In the ancient Middle Eastern world, to meditate meant to ponder deeply, but it also included speaking. In this it is much like prayer, or *oratio*. But there is another capacity that is important to us here. It is the faculty of imagination.

When we meditate, the fathers encourage us to use our imagination. St. Bonaventure says to "imagine vividly" when recalling the stories and scenes of Scripture. This happens naturally whether we like it or not. When we think, we visualize in pictures. We see images as soon as we think a thought. That is how the brain works. When we read about Jesus, we usually see a picture of him as we imagine him. Even when we think in abstract thought, we see pictures of numbers and ideas in our mind's eye. To meditate is to cultivate this with the assistance of the Spirit without getting obsessive about it.

When we read about Jesus, we should allow an image of Jesus to arise naturally. We should allow that image to be beautiful and friendly. It is important to rid ourselves of false images that may see him as a harsh judge and such. Often these images were put into our mind by well-meaning but somewhat misguided teachers in our youth.

When I first visited the Holy Land, I experienced a wonderful help in my biblical meditations. By walking the land where Jesus walked and getting to know the culture related to the culture of Jesus, I was able to meditate more vividly about Jesus. After going there, I can recall the actual feel of the Middle Eastern sand between my toes as I walked the Judean desert and the bustle of the "souk," the covered markets in the narrow streets and alleys of Jerusalem, Nazareth, or other Middle Eastern cities and villages. I can see and smell the freshness of the Galilean hills and fields when the winter rains bring out the red poppy-like "lilies of the field" referred to by Jesus. I can feel the calm of the shepherd in the field outside of Bethlehem in Shepherd's Field, where I once stayed in a hermit's cave overnight. I can also get the feel of the ancient Palestinian monks after walking from St. George's monastery down the Wadi Kelt between Jerusalem and Jericho where there were once thousands of hermits living in the caves in the cliffs along the wadi, or dry riverbed. These things all added content to my imagination as I meditated on the life of Jesus and the first monks of the Palestinian desert.

These images also stir up our other faculties. As I visualize these things, I can remember how they felt and smelled. This stirs up emotions of the heart. While there was sometimes some discomfort in those journeys, they are mainly wonderful stirrings for me.

Meditation also guides our emotions and senses. Left to themselves, senses and emotions can run wild and begin to rule our life instead of empowering it. We become slaves to our senses and experiences of emotional highs and lows. Right meditation is based on truth, which is like the rudder of the ship of our spiritual life.

Jesus says, "Wherever your treasure lies, there will you find your heart" (Luke 12:34). If we make our treasure meditating on the good things of God found in Scripture and tradition, we will find that our unruly emotions and senses will begin to almost naturally settle down. There will still be tests and temptations, but we will have found a key that is a great aid to guiding the rest of our life to the things of God.

Another aspect of meditation is the direction of the mind. But to direct it we often have to empty it first of the cacophony of images and ideas that fill it from our disordered lives. The disordered mind plays an almost constant movie of the things that happen to us in life. Many have trouble focusing on any one thing because of this constant mental noise. This is sometimes called "monkey mind" because thoughts jump around in our mind liked a caged monkey that cannot stay still. So, we usually need to still the mind before we can fill it with good thoughts and direct it and the rest of our energies and active faculties.

Meditation is a creative use of the imagination that stirs the senses, emotions, and thoughts. It is a most important stage in our prayer life. It creatively uses body and soul to lead us to union with God. But many people stop with meditation. There is much more.

Contemplatio

Contemplation goes beyond meditation that uses thoughts, senses, and emotions to a pure spiritual union with God beyond all phenomenal perceptions. It is a union of Essence to essence, Spirit to spirit, and Being to being. It is beyond all phenomenal energies, forms, concepts, or ideas. It is pure spiritual union with the One Who Is. In it the human spirit is reborn, awakened, and rediscovered in the Spirit of God. It then becomes the primary faculty of our human being where all is intuitively known and experienced in God.

After it is experienced, the other faculties do not go away, nor do we cease using *lectio, oratio,* or *meditatio.* They become the pathways to *contemplatio.* They are only important in light of the experience of pure contemplative union with God. They are not the end. They are the means to the end. The end is contemplative union with God.

But this does not mean that they are unimportant or should be discontinued once the contemplative grace has been received. To stop the other practices would eventually lead to a drifting away from the very things that bring us closer to God. It would be like saying to one's spouse that romantic dinners and such are no longer important. They are! In fact, they continue to lead the healthy couple into a pure conjugal union that is beyond all such preliminary experiences. Granted, once the union is consummated such things take on a new meaning, but they never cease having importance. In fact they take on a much deeper significance once the pure union is experienced. They now become the ongoing discipline and ritual that usher us into the contemplative experience more easily than ever before. Like a well-trodden pathway to a love's home, we come to know the path and look forward to it because it takes us to our desired end. We actually begin to long for it because we know to where the path leads. Likewise, the disciplines of *lectio, oratio,* and *meditatio* become all the richer and more longed for after the contemplative experience to which they led in the first place.

But they do take on a different character. They only make sense in light of the contemplative experience. Before contemplation, they were the greatest grace we knew from God. After contemplation, they are only the means to God, not the pure experience of God.

In some traditions this has led to a complete jettisoning of the disciplines that lead to the experience. The Hindu sannyasi are released from the obligations of ritual worship and sacrifice once they profess the sannyasi vow. This would be like giving up participation in the Eucharist or Sunday worship once we taste the contemplative grace. We don't.

The Christian tradition comes closest to this regarding the monastic obligation of praying the Psalter after experiencing the contemplative grace as a strict recluse or hermit. At that time we only pray the psalms to catapult us into contemplation. Once we make that jump, we stop praying the Psalter and simply enter into contemplative silence. But the monastic tradition does not recommend that those still in cenobitical community absent themselves from daily common prayer. As Hebrews says, "We should not absent ourselves from the assembly, as some do, but encourage one another, and this all the more because you see that The Day draws near" (Heb 10:25).

So, the stages of *lectio, oratio, meditatio,* and *contemplatio* work together in succession, and each enriches the one before as we move forward. When we refer to *lectio* in monastic tradition, we are really referring to the entire process. Those in the new monasticism should value this tradition as most precious in the spiritual journey. Indeed, the communities of the new monasticism are there to provide support for those who make that journey. That is one of the most important reasons that they exist at all.

Texts

Within the topic of the universal monk, the question of texts for *lectio* is a good one. Originally, Origen was referring to a prayerful reading of the Bible. Later, the Christian tradition added reading the monastic and church fathers and saints as well. As things developed in the Christian East, the Hesychast tradition recommended reading the fathers first in order to have a right interpretation of the Scriptures. The interfaith dimension encourages one to be firmly rooted in one's own tradition before branching out into another's in order to avoid getting uprooted, groundless, and confused. These are all most helpful insights.

At the trial of Jesus Christ, Pilate asked, "What is truth?" This is still a good question. Plus, how do we get it?

The first thing is that "truth" has a variety of meanings. We shall mention two meanings that were taught to me by some of the translators of the New International Version of the Bible. I was just beginning my ministry and was fresh into the Jesus Movement and I took a rather fundamentalist approach to the Bible. The translators were asked about the word "truth." They surprised us with a most mystical explanation. They said that it refers primarily to "reality" and is intended to mean union with God as the Eternal Truth.

As I have pondered their and other scholarly teachers' explanations, I have reached the following conclusions thus far: Truth refers to objective truth, as in something being true or false. But it also means "reality" and refers to the things that are beyond the illusory truths to those that are eternal. In religion, the first refers to objective doctrine about faith and morality. The second refers to the mystical experience of the spiritual and the divine. One is known primarily with the head and branches out from there to one's senses, emotions, and intuitions. The other is known primarily on the level of spiritual intuition beyond logic and branches out to renew the mind with greater clarity, the emotions with greater enthusiasm, and the senses with greater sharpness and health.

For the Catholic Christian, we try to stay in touch with the organic spiritual process from which we get the story of the life and ministry of Jesus Christ. What is most important for the Christian is to be in touch with the historical Jesus and the cosmic Christ, or Jesus Christ. We believe that Jesus is the Word Incarnate and that he passed on his primary teachings to his apostles, who in turn passed them on through successors. Plus, a monastic and mystical heritage developed within and alongside the apostolic tradition that continually renews it and helps reform it whenever such reform is necessary. This presents us with a vast resource for spiritual reading for *lectio divina*.

The relation between Catholic and Orthodox mystical writings is interesting here. There have been independent developments since the schism of 1054. In recent decades Catholics and Protestants have expressed interest in the Jesus Prayer and the Hesychast tradition. At first, the Orthodox were not in favor of Catholics using these texts, based on the premise that good doctrine must precede good mysticism, and they do not agree with our doctrine. Indeed, Catholics have been hesitant to accept the Hesychastic distinction between divine uncreated energies and essence, since Aquinas said that each is in the other. But recently the more progressive Orthodox have agreed that Orthodox and Catholics substantially agree on the great bulk of doctrine, so it was OK for us to explore this tradition. But they rightly maintain that the spirituality of the East, especially as seen in the *Philokalia*, is linked essentially to being under the guidance of the spiritual father or mother. There has been great sharing and dialogue since this was opened up.

We are open to other non-Catholic texts, ranging from Anglican to Anabaptist to Protestant. Most of this body of work is more theological and social in character, but much still treats what contemplatives would consider more active prayer. While real devotional literature is not as evident in Protestant tradition, it is not altogether absent. Andrew Murray and Dietrich Bonhoeffer are examples of authors of great texts successfully used by some today. Many have also used the later classics like the powerful "God Calling" with great success. The modern trend in this tradition is for more devotional and self-help handbooks that deal with practical daily living as a Christian.

Sources beyond the Hebrew Scriptures from which Christianity was birthed pose a unique situation. Within the Bible, a certain hierarchy of divine revelation exists, with the gospels holding the preeminent place, followed by the rest of the New Testament, and finally the Old Testament, or Hebrew Scriptures. The fathers and ecumenical councils would come next, then all the writings of the great doctors and saints. After that, many interested in interfaith spirituality have begun reading the sources of other religions for personal inspiration as well as for mere scholarly ends.

Vatican II recognizes that the Spirit of God has inspired the scriptures of other faiths and that God has revealed his truth and love through them but not in a complete and inerrant way. They contain revelation but not formal Revelation. They are inspired but not formally Inspired. Therefore, they cannot be taken uncritically. They must be discerned through the lens of Christian revelation in the Scriptures and apostolic tradition as interpreted through the church, from which Scripture and tradition came.

This interpretive lens is an inescapable part of the process. Any practitioners of any other faith will read our Christian Scriptures through the lens of their own faith tradition. We cannot help but see any faith other than our own through the lens of our own culture and religion. It is inescapable.

It is also recommended. We tend to be interested in interfaith texts at the beginning of our conversion from other religions to Christ and again after we have been fully grounded in the Christian faith for many years. While we are being theologically and doctrinally grounded, it is usually best to stay focused on the sacred Christian texts more exclusively. Otherwise, it is simply too easy to get your head turned around, your mind confused, your emotions and even your senses agitated, and your spirit clouded to the point that real contemplation is nearly impossible except by God's grace. During formation in our community, I usually recommend staying almost exclusively with Scripture, the fathers, and the monastic and Franciscan sources. This keeps one focused. After years of that stability, it might be one's calling to branch out more into interfaith meditations during *lectio*.

But it is wonderful that in time those who are called to do so can find inspiration from all these great religious sources for *lectio*. I have carried pocket versions of most of the scriptures and sacred texts from most of the major religions of the world with me whenever I travel. I find great inspiration and solace in them, even though I also carry my Bible, Franciscan writings, and Rule of St. Benedict as my primary Christian and monastic readings. Plus, since the advent of e-books, I carry a veritable library of religious scriptures and sacred texts with me wherever I go. Keeping Jesus and Catholic Christianity central to my faith experience, I am free to use them for *lectio* as well.

So, go find a great spiritual book and read. But do more than merely read. Pray and read. You will be entering into *lectio*. Let the words evoke images, and let the images conjure up senses and smells. Feel. Then settle back down to silence in simply being what you read. Let your mind take you to a place beyond the mind, emotions, or senses. This is the place of pure spiritual intuition. Then you will be doing *lectio*.

Common Prayer
The Liturgy of the Hours

Meditation is not just individual. It is also communal. The church is a body of believers that are the Body of Christ on earth, the People of God, who enjoy a communion with Jesus and each other. This immediately brings us to the experience of liturgy. In addition to celebrating the Eucharist, monastic communities also prayed the Liturgy of the Hours in common from a very early date.

Today people are rediscovering the Liturgy of the Hours. They are hungry for some order in their prayer lives that simply praying according to the inspiration of the moment sometimes misses. Plus, as we face a priest shortage in the Catholic Church, we are being encouraged to pray the Liturgy of the House when Mass cannot be celebrated. The monks of old and the cathedral tradition of the early church give us the foundation for this venerable practice. The monks call it simply "The Work of God."

I come out of the Jesus Movement. We started with very little or nothing regarding forms and orders of worship. We prayed spontaneously. We read Scripture as the Lord, or our own needs, led us. When the Spirit was moving, this was a very wonderful way to pray and read. When we were in dry times, it often became very stagnant. The same thing seemed to happen in the charismatic renewal and still occurs in non-denominational expressions of Christianity. To rectify this situation, we have seen the publishing of Bibles and prayer books like *The One Year Bible*. It has been helpful. We have also seen a resurgence of interest in liturgical prayer as an aid in praying throughout the day and year in an intentional manner.

A similar development has happened in the new monasticism movement. The 24-7 Boiler Rooms of Europe witnessed young people filling the prayer time with prayer in music, poetry, drama, and dance. Soon a liturgy of sorts developed. When the movement developed a communal expression, it used the Rule of St. Benedict as its guide, and liturgy became more important.

This is also how liturgy developed in the early church and monasticism. People wanted to pray alone and together. The early church fathers relate how at first they prayed the Our Father three times a day, morning, noon, and night. They celebrated the Lord's Supper, which they called "the Eucharist" or "the thanksgiving," at least once a week on the day of Jesus' resurrection, Sunday. They also began praying the psalms every day in their places of worship.

The Liturgy of the Hours was first prayed in two settings, the cathedral and the monastic. The cathedral setting was usually prayed thematically under the direction of a deacon and/or the local bishop. It was sung in a style that alternated between a leader, called a cantor, and the congregation, much like today's responsorial psalms.

The monastic setting was prayed more meditatively as one or two monks read the psalms straight through numerically; the other monks listened attentively while making ropes. They prayed all 150 psalms daily.

At first, the monks of St. Antony of the Desert lived in greater solitude throughout the week and only came together once a week for the *synaxis*, or gathering prayer, on Saturday, with a Eucharist on Sunday before they went back into the solitude of their hermitages. Monastic common prayer was first used by the Pachomian monks, who lived in daily contact with one another and prayed together at various times throughout the day.

The Rule of St. Benedict legislated an approach to common prayer, called the Work of God, that has become the model for monks of the West. The rule integrated the cathedral and monastic models. It uses a common approach to praying the psalms together that is thematic like the cathedral but retains the autonomy of the monastic from the diocesan church. It also mitigates the 150 daily psalms to a weekly cycle. There is an emphasis on quality rather than quantity. Of course, they prayed the Office in their churches or oratories. Today, monasteries retain the autonomy to put together their own exact cycle of psalms but base all such customs on the spirit of the rule.

The Franciscans and other mendicants who arose in the thirteenth century were itinerant ministers and traveled throughout the world and found that even this was difficult to do. First, they were exempted from having to pray the Office in a church, though this was always preferable. Also, the complete monastic Office required rather large books, and they were simply too much to carry as most of the friars walked on foot like the poor of the day. So they developed a brief version of the Office called the Breviary. As the friars "carpeted Europe," as Dante said, they naturally spread the use of the Breviary throughout the church in the West.

Other developments in the Divine Office are also relevant. Some communities arose who were so active in ministry that they were exempted from praying the Breviary in community. The Jesuits are a good example of this. They are required to pray the Office but may do so individually. Today, this same exemption also applies to any religious who find themselves traveling alone. But prayer with others in community is still the preferred way to pray the common prayer of a community or church.

The Rule of Benedict sets a high spiritual standard for the actual practice of the Office. In chapter 19 it says:

> We believe that the divine presence is everywhere and *that in every place the eyes of the Lord are watching the good and the wicked* (Prov. 15:3). But beyond the least doubt we should believe this to be especially true when we celebrate the divine office. . . . Let us consider, then, how we ought to behave in the presence of God and his angels, and let us stand to sing the psalms in such a way that our minds are in harmony with our voices. (RB19.1-2, 6-7)

It continues in chapter 20 :

> We must know that God regards our purity of heart and tears of compunction, not our many words. Prayer should therefore be short and pure, unless perhaps it is prolonged under the inspiration of divine grace. In community, however, prayer should always be brief; and when the superior gives the signal, all should rise together. (RB 20.3-5)

Most believe that this "shortness" refers not so much to the length of the Office itself but to the collects or collection prayers prayed out loud after the psalms. They were probably prayed spontaneously in those days. In other words, do not go on and on in spontaneous prayer. We have all suffered under those who monopolize such situations. It is never entirely fun!

The musical setting in the Rule of Benedict is not certain. We do not know exactly when they began to chant the psalms, but we know they started to do so at a very early date. The musical style developed according to their culture. In the East, chant was always more Eastern and to this day sounds more like the modes and tones we hear from an Islamic minaret than what our Western ears are accustomed to. Gregorian chant unfolded slowly in the West, using eight tones instead of major or minor keys as we are used to hearing in modern music. While we try to preserve the spirit and form of Gregorian chant today, more modern tones are an appropriate development of the sung monastic tradition as well. Most monasteries use a combination of the two.

In the twentieth century the ecumenical monks of Taize, France, further developed the monastic office by using a monthly cycle for all 150 psalms and their own beautiful musical settings that are at once both contemporary and ancient. This had an effect on the modern Catholic Liturgy of the Hours that also uses a monthly cycle for the 150 psalms, excluding some of the more violent psalms that are sometimes difficult to understand in relation to the nonresistance of Jesus.

It is interesting that so many new monastic and quasi-monastic communities outside of the Catholic faith are also finding great help with the Liturgy of the Hours. Many struggle to find ways to pray the Scriptures as communities and to find a way to go through Scripture in anything other than a haphazard manner. Some resort to going straight through and praying the psalms numerically, but most find this tedious. The established Liturgy of the Hours and daily readings from Mass present a great answer to this search that is already established by centuries of successful tradition and much contemporary scholarship. Why try to reinvent the wheel?

But it is not enough just to get the formula down. The correct *ordo* (a guide to the right dates and psalms, readings, intercessions, and prayers) never saved anyone! We must also pray the Liturgy of the Hours with the right spirit. As St. Thomas Aquinas said, we must do the "right thing rightly" in order for it to be spiritually fruitful and accomplish God's will in religion. Religion for religion's sake is just vain religion.

In our new monastic community we encourage a balanced integration of the charismatic and the contemplative, the spontaneous and the liturgical, in our praying of the Liturgy of the Hours. We use a rather traditional setting of psalm tones that are usually chanted with or without instrumental accompaniment with guitar or keyboard. Usually, however, we prefer it a cappella. We sing them rather slowly, as we do with all recitations of the liturgical texts, but not laboriously. We keep our singing and responses slow enough to be meaningful but fast enough to be lively. It is "sung speech." After each psalm we pause for some silence. At that point we allow one or two lines or phrases to be repeated back by individual monastics in choir to voice what the Spirit is doing on the spot in the membership of the community. We are, however, careful not to abuse the silence with personal agendas and such. Most visitors feel that our liturgical practice is most beautiful and spiritually life-giving. It easily stands on a par with, or even surpasses for some, the best of other monastic chants.

Our domestic members are encouraged to pray the Liturgy of the Hours individually or together as often as they can. We do not obligate them to pray it daily, but we do encourage it. The Liturgy of the Hours is the official prayer of the Latin Rite of the Roman Catholic Church. It stands second only to the Mass. It is to be preferred to any private devotion like the rosary, the Stations of the Cross, the *Angelus*, the Jesus Prayer, novenas, or any other private prayers. All these things are commendable and are encouraged, but they are not given the same priority as the Liturgy of the Hours.

Today, the Liturgy of the Hours is a great way to pray the Psalter and other biblical texts in an orderly way that allows for a Spirit-filled participation. Especially when priests are less available for daily Mass, the Liturgy of the Hours is a wonderful way to remain in touch with the praying church.

The Roman Liturgy of the Hours is more than the prayers of a specific monastic community or religious family. It is the official prayer of the entire Catholic Church. There is a principle with the Liturgy of the Hours that is quite powerful for those who understand it. It is bigger than the ups and downs of one's personal prayer life. It is even bigger than the ups and downs of a specific monastic or religious community. These things all rise and fall pretty easily, depending on what is going on in the life of an individual or specific community. The Liturgy of the Hours brings the stability of the universal church to an individual or community. It is greatly stabilizing, especially in times of trouble.

Many times when I am simply too tired or discouraged to come up with my own creative way to pray, the Liturgy of Hours gives me direction and encouragement that is bigger than my own experience. It allows me to experience God in a way much bigger than myself alone. It keeps me encouraged and strengthened by God through his people on earth in the church. This has been one of God's great gifts to me.

The other thing that has been a great personal gift to me is how the Scripture has soaked into me through praying the Liturgy of the Hours almost daily for over thirty years. Hearing the word of God in the liturgy repeatedly has allowed the Scriptures to slowly and almost imperceptibly soak into my soul. Without even trying to, I have memorized Scripture in a way that I could never have done through any memorization technique. I am most grateful for this wonderful gift.

I encourage you to make it a regular part of your life as well. It will be a blessing to you from God if you learn to pray it properly and prayerfully.

Many ask how to get started. There are some good books out there on how to pray the Liturgy of the Hours. It is also available online. These are most helpful. But the best way to learn to pray the Office is to pray it personally with a gathered community of faith. One of the best places to experience this is in a monastery that chants the Office prayerfully, reverently, and beautifully. The Benedictines offer a great environment for this. But they do not use the formal Roman Rite of the Liturgy of the Hours. They use their own rite specific to their own community and/or congregation. The later communities, like the Franciscans, use the formal Roman Rite of the Liturgy of the Hours, but they often recite it too fast. So I recommend learning the spirit of the Office from the Benedictines and the Roman form of it from a later community like the Franciscans, Carmelites, Augustinians, or Dominicans. Of course, we cordially invite you to join us at Little Portion Hermitage anytime! I think we have put the best of both worlds together pretty well.

A Walk through the Liturgy

We have already discussed the biblical human anthropology of spirit, soul, and body as presented by St. Paul in 1 Thessalonians 5. Due to the presence of sin in this world, this order has been reversed to body, soul, and spirit. The body and soul represent senses, emotions, and thoughts. The spirit is the deepest essence of the human being and, though the most real part of who we are, is beyond a complete grasp by our senses, emotions, or thoughts.

The eucharistic liturgy takes us through the externals of our human being in the senses, emotions, and thoughts of body and soul to the deepest part of who we are as human spirit in God's Spirit in a way that is purely mystical, a mystery, or a sacrament. This is especially true in the sacrament of the Eucharist.

The earliest monastic tradition indicates that the Eucharist was very important to the monks of the desert but was not a daily practice. In the semi-eremitical tradition of St. Antony of the Desert or St. Macarius (c. AD 330–91), the monks would live in isolated cells in solitude throughout the week. On Saturday they would walk a day's walk to a common center where they would pray the *synaxis* prayers and celebrate an *agape* feast. On Sunday morning they would celebrate the Mass together, gather their supplies for the coming week, and walk back to their isolated hermit cells. Consequently, a weekly Mass on Sundays seems to have been the norm.

St. Pachomius of the Desert founded a more strictly communal expression of monasticism where the monks lived and prayed together every day. In the tradition of St. Pachomius there is little or no evidence of a communal Mass. It is simply understood as part of the overall early Christian worship experience.

Likewise, the Rule of St. Benedict says little about the Mass. It accepts priests into the community on the condition that they do not become puffed up or proud due to their clerical rank. It allows them to say the final blessing but only with the permission of the abbot, who was more than likely a lay monk. It does mention "communion," but it is not entirely clear as to whether that is a Mass or Communion service.

The Rule of the Master, which probably predates the Rule of St. Benedict by several decades, is very explicit, however, about the Communion service. It indicates that the monks would celebrate a daily Communion service in the monastery presided over by the abbot and would go to the local parish on Sundays and special feast days.

This brief overview shows that the eucharistic liturgy and Communion services were important parts of the early monastic tradition. While early monasticism was a predominantly lay movement that prophetically spoke to and challenged the diocesan church, it was not opposed to the diocesan church. It existed as a renewal within and alongside the more typical diocesan expression of Christianity.

So let's take a walk through the liturgy and journey from the senses, emotions, and thoughts of body and soul to the realm of spirit, the place of mystery, beyond sensual grasp, emotional capacity, or intellectual understanding, in a way that builds on and enlivens them all.

Let's begin with the senses of the body. Common worship is, by its nature, a sensual experience. The first thing we have to do is leave our homes and places of employment and come to church! We have to gather physically in one place. That place is a church building, and the building is physical. We park a physical car in a physical parking lot, walk in physical bodies on physical legs, and enter through a physical door into the church building. Even monastics have to leave their cells and gather together in church!

We begin to use our senses to get us into a spiritual place of worship. In most Roman Catholic churches we almost immediately dip our hands into holy water and make the sign of the cross. These are physical gestures using physical elements blessed by God through the prayers of the church. Next, we make our way to a place to sit, usually in a church pew, chair, or monastic choir stall. Before sitting down, we bow reverently to the altar or an icon (in Eastern Rite churches) and genuflect to the King of Kings in the reserved Blessed Sacrament. These are all physical gestures, movements, and things made holy through prayer and the Spirit.

We also notice other physical things in the church building. We see stained-glass windows and awe-inspiring architecture. We make use of "smells and bells" to aid us in our worship of God. All of this affirms that God works through creation to draw people to himself who is both in and beyond creation.

Almost immediately on experiencing these physical things, our thoughts and our emotions are involved in the process. The human being is a united being that cannot be separated strictly into sections and parts. As soon as we experience the physical reality, we immediately process it with thoughts, which in turn stir and direct the emotions. This takes us from the realm of body to soul, from senses to thoughts and emotions.

If we understand holy water correctly, it reminds us of dying to the old self and being raised up as a new creation in

Christ. Dipping our hands in holy water and making the sign of the cross emphasize this mystical reality as soon as we walk through the church door. Uplifting architecture and beautiful works of art in stained glass and statuary lift our hearts and minds from and through the mundane to the supernatural, the ordinary to the extraordinary, and the practical to the mystical. This is a wonderful exercise in the incarnational reality of God in our lives!

Next we begin to sing. I am a composer and singer of sacred songs, so this is very close to my heart. All too often the singing in Catholic churches is an exercise in mumbling songs that we don't really like and barely know. But that's not what singing is supposed to be! It's supposed to stir our hearts and minds through beautiful melodies and profound lyrics into the presence of God.

My song "Come Worship the Lord" gives some basic directions in the first two words of the title as to how to worship God. The first word is "come." This means that when we worship God we must be willing to leave our safety zones and come forward to follow Jesus. Jesus never allows us to stand still in our walk with him. If we do this, our spiritual life, as well as our sacred sensual, emotional, and intellectual life, will stagnate, dry up, and die. We must always be willing to come forward when we follow Jesus authentically.

The next word is "worship." When we worship, we must be willing to exalt God over everything we are, the good and the bad, the successes and failures, the hopes and dreams and fears. The Scriptures say the Lord is enthroned on the praises of his people. I do not claim to fully understand that, but I know that's what the Scriptures say.

Do we really enthrone the Lord on our singing at the opening song at Mass? I'm afraid not! Most of the time we just mumble along in an exercise that is vain repetition at worst and halfhearted, lukewarm worship at best.

Authentic worship and praise is an upward motion of the spirit to God. It is a complete letting go of self that is uninhibited and passionate, including the senses of the human body, as well as the mind and emotions. We energetically let go of our self and throw ourselves out and up to God as if in a biblical "wave offering."

The use of song, which stirs senses, emotions, and thoughts, continues as we enter into the penitential rite and the Gloria. In the penitential rite we allow ourselves to pass beyond all logic-driven conversion in attrition and to the conversion of the heart based on personal love relationship with Jesus in contrition. This is often a much overlooked and rushed part of our contemporary liturgy. Immediately following the absolution granted to us in the penitential rite, we explode into a song of jubilation and gratitude in the Gloria.

After the opening prayer we enter into the Liturgy of the Word. This is an intentional journey from senses and emotions to the mind of Christ. Having focused and purified our senses and emotions in the opening of the liturgy, we can now hear the word of God without distraction. The Scriptures are solemnly proclaimed, and we prayerfully listen. The Liturgy of the Word includes not only the solemn proclamation of the Scriptures but the homily as well! This means that the deacon or priest is not just preaching his personal opinion about the teaching of the church and the Word of God. This also means that we should listen to the homily attentively. Far too often we fidget and look at our watches if the homilist dares to go more than ten minutes!

I remember a story from our local parish of St. Anne's in Berryville, Arkansas. The bishop had assigned a new priest there. After a few weeks I asked him how he was doing. He responded that the parishioners said he preached too long in his homilies and that he should not go for more than ten minutes. I commented that his homilies were only twelve or thirteen minutes long. (Notice that I knew how long he preached, indicating that I was timing him too!) When he asked them why they wanted him to keep them so short, they responded that if the homily was too long, by the time they got to the restaurant in the local bowling alley after church, the Baptists had already gotten there and beat them to the best food! Humorous as this story is, we should allow our ordained ministers, who have been trained to preach, to bring the word of God to us without inhibition or impatience on our part. After all, isn't the food of the word of God more important than bodily food?

After this we make a solemn profession of our faith and pray for the needs of our brothers and sisters within the community. Petitions ask God for his love and mercy for those in need. Intercessions mean that we are willing to stand in their place even as Jesus stands in our place as we ask God to bring his love, mercy, and healing to those most in need of his mercy at the very moment we offer these prayers. Petitioning is most commendable. Intercession is truly profound and a gift that can only be called Christlike and divine.

Up until now we have journeyed through the senses, emotions, and thoughts of body and soul. This is a most awe-inspiring journey and one that we rarely take full advantage of within our liturgy. But there is more, much more!

I am reminded of my good friend Michael Card, who described his worship experience at a Bible church in Nashville. This is a church where some of the best singers and musicians from contemporary Christian music regularly go to worship when they are in town on Sunday. The music is extraordinary. They sing with great emotion and talent and with great understanding of the lyrical content. It is heavenly! Then they move into a great Bible teaching by a great Bible scholar and preacher, who is also a great motivational speaker. He calls people to give their lives completely to Jesus Christ, and many respond every week. Then they pray with heartfelt intercessions for those in need. The entire service is quite moving. Then there is a closing benediction, and they all go home.

The problem is that they do all the great preparation work in worship but then never go to the goal of mystical union with Christ beyond senses, emotions, and thoughts. As Mike told me once, "I feel like I've gone through the entire marriage ceremony, and never got to kiss the bride!"

In the Catholic Mass we get to kiss the bride! After the procession, penitential rite, Gloria, opening prayer, Liturgy of the Word, creed, and intercessions, we move to the high point of the liturgy: the Liturgy of the Eucharist. This is what all the rest has been building up to.

In the Liturgy of the Eucharist we move beyond senses, emotions, and thoughts of body and soul into a pure mystical union of spirit with Jesus that occurs through and beyond them all. This mystical union with Jesus is spirit to Spirit, essence to Essence, and being to Being that is beyond anything we can fully grasp with the phenomenal human faculties of senses, emotions, or thoughts. This is the "source and summit" of the entire Christian life. It is the reason for all that has come before, and he gives life to all that has come before.

But there is more. This contemplative, mystical union with Jesus is something that we must do personally, but it is greater than a mere private experience. This is something we do together. It is a communal experience of pure contemplation!

It is often said that Catholics don't have altar calls. And it is true that most Catholics have never experienced coming forward to the altar in the way it is done in a revival meeting or even an evangelical church. But let it not be said that Catholics don't have altar calls! At every Mass we have the opportunity to come forward and to give our life to Jesus at the greatest ongoing sacrament or call that we can experience not only personally but also as a gathered people. It is at once deeply personal and communal. It is private and public all at once.

At the time of Communion we move beyond all that has come before. It is no longer important whether the ushers and the people were friendly, whether the singing was good or bad, or whether the preaching was engaging or downright dull. These things are all important, but they are not the most important reason that we come to Mass. We come for Jesus and Jesus alone. The liturgy may have been terrible, but I figure that if Jesus shows up, so can I! And the fact of the matter is that Jesus does, in fact, show up every time.

When we go forward to receive Jesus in the Eucharist, we are coming forward to the greatest ongoing sacramental altar call that we can do together as a united people. It is the most powerful of all alter calls. When we go forward, we are standing up for Jesus, leaving our comfort zones, and giving our lives entirely to Christ in the love response to him who first gave his life entirely for each one of us personally and as a united community of faith. We do this not out of compulsion or out of law but purely out of love. It is a free act that far surpasses every act of religious law or legal obligation.

Now if your last Communion was not such an experience for you, do not feel too guilty. We Catholics have enough guilt already! But make a little promise that the next time you go forward to receive Jesus in the Eucharist you will give your life entirely to him, and it will be for you a sacramental altar call that can be rivaled by no other.

Likewise, as you experience your next Mass, enter fully into every dimension of the liturgy with all that you are: spirit, soul, and body. Allow your senses, emotions, thoughts, and the intuitions of the spirit to fully experience and participate in this wonderful miracle of God, this gift given to us out of love by the God of love. Enter fully into every gesture, every song, every response, every Scripture, every prayer from the early church, and most especially into the greatest Mystery of mysteries, the true presence of Jesus in the most holy Eucharist.

Then the entire liturgy will become for us a corporate experience of praise and worship, inspiring motivation, deep meditation, profound prayer, and mystical union with Christ. It will become something that we no longer "have to do" but something we have the privilege to do!

Almost without exception, the communities of the New Monasticism are rediscovering this vibrancy in not only the Liturgy of the Hours, but also in the celebration of the Eucharist. This is true not only of new Catholic monastic communities but also of those from other traditional and new expressions of Christianity, as well as some who are more interfaith in their membership. This renewed vibrancy in the celebration of the liturgy is, in and of itself, an outreach of the new evangelization spoken of by Pope John Paul II to all people everywhere. As the saying goes, "Good liturgy builds faith, and bad liturgy destroys faith." A return to the original vibrancy of the liturgy builds the faith of everyone who participates. This is a great work of the New Monasticism in the new evangelization!

Obedience

Obedience is often thought of in terms of having to do what others tell you to do whether you like it or not. We think of it in terms of a rather military approach or the worst memories of obeying parents when we were convinced that they did not understand or were just plain wrong. These are very negative images that make the whole idea of obedience very difficult for the average person.

While there is a functional aspect to religious obedience, it really does not tell the whole story. For the monastic tradition, obedience is a spirituality based on listening that becomes a whole way of life. We learn to really listen before we respond, and we learn to respond instead of react. There is a big difference. This means that we can be helpful in responding to religious and secular leadership, to the church, to humanity, and to all creation. It is a spirituality that brings freedom and life to all.

The Rule of St. Benedict says:

> Listen carefully, my son, to the master's instructions, and attend to them with the ear of your heart. This is advice from a father who loves you; welcome it, and faithfully put it into practice. The labor of obedience will bring you back to him from whom you had drifted through the sloth of disobedience. . . .
>
> Therefore we intend to establish a school for the Lord's service. In drawing up its regulations, we hope to set down nothing

harsh, nothing burdensome. The good of all concerned, however, may prompt us to a little strictness in order to amend faults and to safeguard love. Do not be daunted immediately by fear and run away from the road that leads to salvation. It is bound to be narrow at the outset. But as we progress in this way of life and in faith, we shall run on the path of God's commandments, our hearts overflowing with the inexpressible delight of love. (RB Prol. 1-2, 45-49)

The prologue of the Rule of St. Benedict begins with an admonition to listening obedience. It ends by establishing a communal support for this obedient listening to God, the church, humanity, and all creation as a way of life. It is a "school of the Lord's service" that is not too harsh and not too lenient. It is a way of doable moderation. It is radical but not fanatical. It brings freedom, not enslavement; life, not death.

The English word "obedience" comes from the root "obey." This comes from the Latin *obedire*, which an overview of English and Latin dictionaries tells us means "obey," "pay attention to," "give ear," literally, "listen to," from *ob* "to" and *audire* "listen, hear." So, attentive listening that gives birth to healthy action is at the root of real obedience.

In Scripture we find a similar idea. In Hebrew the word *Shama* means "to listen attentively," "discern," and "to tell." In the New Testament the letter to the Hebrews says that Jesus "learned obedience from his suffering." The word used there is *hypakoē*, pronounced "hoop-ak-o-ay'," and means attentive hearkening and, by implication, compliance or submission. Again, the root is to listen attentively.

This listening obedience forms the core of the Benedictine monastic spirituality. It is a school of the Lord's service whereby one learns to quiet the inner cacophony of sensual, emotional, and mental noise through real prayer and meditation. This spiritual state is achieved and maintained through a balanced life of personal *lectio divina* and communal prayer.

Other good methods of meditation are also encouraged. This silences the inner turmoil of our lives and allows us to really listen so that we can properly respond to the needs of life externally.

But there is an external aspect to obedience. If the inner life is silenced and properly focused and directed, so is the external life. Religious communities must function. This requires external manifestations of obedience. Leaders have the duty to arrange the life of the community personally or through delegates.

The BSC Way of Life says:

> The priorities of community life are as follows:
> 1) God is first.
> 2) The church comes next as an umbrella governing every aspect of our life on earth.
> 3) Within the umbrella of the church comes the nuclear family and the monastic and domestic community.
>   a. The nuclear family composes what the church calls the most basic expression of God's ordained natural community for humanity and the domestic church.
>   b. For celibate monastic members, the monastic community becomes their primary family circle, as in any traditional community of consecrated life.
>   c. For the monastic and domestic single and family members, the community becomes the privileged place for nurturing the family.
> 4) Finally comes the local church of the diocese and parish.
> 5) From the church, we overflow to minister to the whole world.

This has some special implications. The first is that we obey God in his mediated authority in the church. The second is the place of the family in an integrated monastic expression. The last is the secular authorities of the world.

Most of this is pretty functional. If we do not have leaders and members, a job simply cannot get done. Even in secular business, if we do not have leaders for the workers, the work will end up in chaos and inefficiency. As much as employees sometimes complain about "the boss," we all know this to be true. A good boss is great for the morale of the employees.

The same thing is true in a community. Without obedience to leaders we cannot get the work of God done on earth. We must have good leaders and good followers. But we cannot have good leaders without good followers. As our BSC Scripture Rule says:

> Heb. 13:17—Obey your leaders and submit to them, for they keep watch over you as men who must render an account. So act so that they may fulfill their task with joy, not with sorrow, for that would be harmful to you.

But this can all sound a bit too functional. The Benedictine tradition gets a bit more personal and close to home. Chapter 5 of the Rule of St. Benedict says, "The first step of humility is unhesitating obedience. . . . [T]hey carry out the superior's order as promptly as if the command came from God himself" (RB 5.1, 4).

This is pretty radical stuff. But it is not enough to simply do what is asked of us. We must do it with the right attitude. Those who come to religious life after time in the military sometimes think that they understand religious obedience. But they often understand it only in part. In the military one obeys because, if you do not, you end up in the brig! So they often obey externally while grumbling in their heart. But they get the job done.

Such external obedience is only half of the story with religious obedience. The RB goes on:

> This very obedience, however, will be acceptable to God and agreeable to men only if compliance with what is commanded is not cringing or sluggish or half-hearted, but free from any grumbling or any reaction of unwillingness. For the obedience

shown to superiors is given to God, as he himself said: *Whoever listens to you, listens to me* (Luke 10:16). Furthermore, the disciples' obedience must be given gladly, for *God loves a cheerful giver* (2 Cor 9:7). If a disciple obeys grudgingly and grumbles, not only aloud but also in his heart, then, even though he carries out the order, his action will not be accepted with favor by God, who sees that he is grumbling in his heart. (RB 5.14-18)

How do we do this? If we think that the obedience is wrong, how can we follow it without objection? Part of the answer is because we believe that God has placed the superior in leadership in our life. This is why the rule says that the abbot stands in the place of Christ and Scripture says that God gives all authority on earth. Obedience to authority is obedience to God. But there is more.

[T]hey are eager to take the narrow road of which the Lord says: *Narrow is the road that leads to life* (Matt 7:14). They no longer live by their own judgment, giving in to their whims and appetites; rather they walk according to another's decisions and directions, choosing to live in monasteries and to have an abbot over them. Men of this resolve unquestionably conform to the saying of the Lord: *I have come not to do my own will, but the will of him who sent me* (John 6:38). (RB 5.11-13)

The real key to understanding monastic obedience is that we are all trying to let go of our dysfunctional will for the will of God. It is not that the human will is wrong. It is rather that we have used our will wrongly and have fallen into habitual negative patterns of the will, and we need some help to get "unstuck."

Submission to the will of an elder or spiritual father or mother is a great way to get some tangible help here on earth. Yes, God is our ultimate help, but it is far too easy to get fooled by our own whims about God when we have no human check and balance right here on earth to help us with heavenly things. That is what a good religious superior is all about. And that is what religious obedience is ultimately for. It is not about some robot-like obedience to a person. It is about learning how to really listen to God.

This does not mean that we will, or even should, always agree with everything that a leader says. They may stand in the place of Christ for us and be established by God, but they are not God. And a good abbot knows all too well that they are certainly not Jesus Christ!

But it does mean that we will have a new attitude toward those in leadership. Instead of arguing with leaders, we will really begin to listen to them. We will respectfully hear them out and be open to their ideas before we present our own. We will love them and see them as friends rather than enemies who must always be resisted. This brings an air of love, respect, and basic human civility to the relationship.

Especially in the United States, we are a ruggedly individualistic people. Part of the very foundation of our nation is based on distrust of predominantly European secular and even religious leaders who oppressed freedom rather than facilitated it. Some of this is good. Some of it can be real obstacle to real spiritual growth.

Individuation is a good thing. Individualism is not. Individuation sees every human life as an unrepeatable gift of God. But it sees the individual against a communitarian backdrop. Creation is a community. Humanity is a community. So is every nation. Churches and monastic communities are that communitarian backdrop in a most special way.

Individualism is good individuation gone bad. It asserts the individual at the expense of the community. It breeds selfish people who are self-obsessed and self-indulgent. It asserts individual rights even at the expense of other's rights. It rolls over anyone and anything that gets in the way of its all-powerful self.

Whether we want to admit it or not, most of us in the United States are affected by this individualistic spirit. Monastic spirituality is a gentle but tough way to get to the heart of this defect and remove it from our life. It is a bit like pulling teeth. Sometimes it hurts right after the extraction. But once removed we are much more comfortable and healthy.

Now these are big ideas with big ramifications. But we have found that these big ideas are usually tested in the little things of community life. Jesus says that if we are found faithful in little things we will be given the great.

We often say that one must learn to "grow a green bean for God" before we can do great things for God. We usually start folks who are physically able in the garden when they enter our monastic community. It has a way of grounding us. It is also a simple work that allows our mind to focus on God while remaining grounded in the simple things of life. It is good for our humility. ("Humble" means to be brought "to the earth.")

Often we are asked to grow that green bean in a way that we do not want to do. Maybe we came from a green bean farm, and think we know a better way. So we go to the head of the farm and tell them about our idea. They listen respectfully, thank us, and then ask us to do it the way we were asked to do it. They have not asked us to do something that is against the teaching of the church on faith and morality or the rule and constitutions of the community. We just don't like it! This sometimes rankles our American pride!

It is right here that we confront our proud, individualistic tendencies. We can learn how to let go of our own self-will, really love and respect our superior, listen to them, and carry out the command. Or we can fall into the typical pattern of arguing. The choice is ours to make. It is our experience that, despite all our high-minded idealism, it is whether or not we can "grow a green bean for God" that decides whether we can remain in a monastic community. Those who can jump this hurdle can stay and prosper in a monastic community. Those who cannot must leave. It may not be their call or their time. But they cannot make it in a monastery if they cannot learn this lesson.

The ultimate lesson of obedience is learning to listen. We listen to God, then we listen to others and all creation. Only when we listen can we really know what to say.

But before we can listen, we must learn how to be still and quiet. To do this we must let go of the old self of constant activity and noise. Remember the pond. We must allow the pond to settle down before we can really see what is in the waters of the soul. As long as the old ego attachments persist, even in the name of religion and God, then we can never see clearly and speak in a way that benefits everyone.

This is what meditation is all about. It is a simple way to be still. We still the body and soul, the senses, emotions, and thoughts, so that the spirit can emerge again through spiritual intuition. Then the thoughts facilitate, the emotions empower, and the senses house this new spiritual life in the Spirit.

But monastic obedience does not stop with the abbot or religious superior. We must learn to really listen to others, to every other brother and sister. In a sense, obedience to the abbot or abbess is just practice for this greater listening obedience to everyone. When we learn obedience to a rule and abbot, then we are ready to live in a listening obedience to God, humanity, the church, our monastic community, and all creation. We begin to live as listeners so that we might really know what to speak and do in our lives. We learn to listen before we speak, share instead of argue, and respond rather than react. This is revolutionary.

One of the greatest tests of this is whether or not we have started formulating our answer before a person has finished speaking to us. We must learn to listen to what a person says before we respond. We must also learn to hear his or her spirit and not only his or her words. Often folks don't communicate well with words. Obedience means to learn to listen, to hear the deepest spirit and soul of another before we respond. Then our response can bring life rather than judgment, anger, and death.

Obedience is a powerful tool to find this new way of listening in an intentional communal environment. It is not about ruling others or submitting ourselves to autocratic leaders. It is a way of spiritual rebirth and liberation. It is a powerful way to be born again. Once that happens, then you are more ready to help others along a similar spiritual journey.

Chastity

We live in one of the most promiscuous cultures on earth. Today, promiscuity is not considered a problem as long as it is between consenting adults. What was once considered pornography has become an accepted norm in the media. The basic fabric of civilization, the traditional family, is breaking down, or at least morphing into something other than what it has almost always been. All that is considered basic Judeo-Christian sexual morality, not to mention most established religions and ancient philosophies of the world, is often being ignored.

Chastity is the remedy for fornication, or sexual sin, the second of the eight vices of early monasticism. This sin comes from the Greek *pornea*, from which we get the English word "pornography." In the Western list of the seven deadly sins, it is usually called "lust." Lust is ego attaching to an otherwise legitimate desire and taking it too far. One of the most common expressions of lust is through sexuality. We call it sexual sin. Fornication is the word that has often been used to generalize all sexual sins, though there are many more forms than strict fornication alone, which, strictly speaking, refers to unlawful sexual intercourse before marriage.

This vice follows gluttony, or giving in to small, almost unnoticeable sensual enticement. But such small concessions can predispose us to greater sensual sins. Lust and sexual sin are the manifestations of such a growing pattern.

The traditional Eastern monastic remedies for interior or external sexual sin of heart, thought, or action is manual labor and vigil. The idea is simply that if you tire your body out through work and get up to pray in the night hours when sexual thoughts often attack, you will solve much of the problem. This actually works pretty well for monks, but it does not go to the deeper problems.

Chastity is one of the positive remedies for lust and sexual sin.

We often think in prohibitive terms when we think of chastity. We think of it in terms of oppression and repression of legitimate sexual desires. We think of it in terms of "can't" and "don't" rather than as a "can do" reality in our life. But this is not really correct. Chastity is a sort of positive gospel poverty whereby we simplify and direct our sexual urges as experienced in thought, desire, and action in healthy and life-giving ways. It is directly related to meditation and contemplation and causes them to grow unhindered, and prosper. It helps us to simplify our life and focus our mind and direct our heart. Chastity is a positive thing, not negative.

"Monk" means "one" and "alone." As we have already learned, this generally means living for God and God alone. It also means supporting one another in a united community in living this radical gospel way of greater silence and solitude for better meditation and contemplative prayer.

This has been predominately applied to celibates. We are clearly "one" and "alone." It also was first applied to hermits for the same reason. But the word was quickly applied to cenobites under St. Pachomius' *koinonia* who lived alone together in community. It can also be applied in an extended fashion to married couples who support one another in living this way of life. This was true primarily with Celtic monasticism and is still true today with today's new integrated monasticism.

For all of us, it is designed to free us up to serve God without distraction. That is really its only purpose. We know that Jesus was a celibate and taught the way of celibacy for those who followed him as a special gift from God (Matt 19:1-12, 25-30). He also blessed marriage at the wedding feast at Cana (John 2:1-11). St. Paul continued this teaching but emphasized that its practical purpose was for freeing one from the responsibilities and secular distractions of raising a family (1 Cor 7).

This might appear rather simplistic to us today, for any priest or monk will tell you that they also have to deal with many of the secular realities of paying bills, meeting the costs of health care and such, and generally existing in this world as much as any family. If they do not have to do so personally, I can guarantee you that their leaders do! But it must also be admitted that married clergy sometimes have to meet the legitimate family responsibilities of spouse and children before they can meet the needs of their congregations and communities. The same is true of married integrated monastic community members. This is as it should be, unless the needs of the family are in direct conflict with the teaching of Jesus and the church. So the celibate line of reasoning still holds true in many cases.

In our integrated monastic community, we apply chastity to mean celibacy for monks and sisters. It also applies to singles before marriage. For married couples, it usually means conjugal chastity where healthy sexual relations within the context of marriage are experienced. We also recognize that some will practice continence, but this is a matter of private choice, not of community policy. We pray that this extra commitment of marital chastity will help keep married members faithful to their spouse for life in a culture where sexual promiscuity and revolving mates has become the norm. This is a great aid in restoring the stability of the Catholic family in a culture where families are falling apart and disintegrating.

The church teaches that there are three things necessary for healthy Christian sexual activity:

1) That it is an expression of *mutual self-giving.* In other words, it is not selfishly motivated but is for the sake of the other. This kind of sexual activity finds itself fulfilled in giving itself completely for the sake of another. It is an act of the self-emptying love of Jesus. This is radically different than the self-gratifying sex of our current sexually promiscuous culture. It is sacramental because it symbolizes and causes the love of Jesus for the church to manifest on earth.

2) That it is *within the context of marriage.* If one completely reveals oneself physically, emotionally, mentally, and spiritually to another, it must be within the context of a committed relationship. Sexual activity is something most sacred and should not be cheaply tossed around from one person to the next. For most of us, this kind of sharing only happens once in a lifetime, because once we have shared it with another, it is for the rest of our life. It takes on the quality of the eternal. It also builds the stability needed for the family in the civilized world.

3) Under ordinary circumstances *children will be produced* from the physical expression of this love union. This is practical as well as mystical. Love is the self-emptying union of two that produces a third. This is trinitarian and is mystical or sacramental. Of course, this does not apply to couples who are not able to have children.

Using the above three points, we can see why the church teaches what she does regarding sexual activity. Pre- and extramarital, homosexual, or self-erotic (masturbatory) activity does not fulfill all three points. But these exclusions should not be understood only as legalistic prohibitions of some kind of puritanical mindset. Rather, it has to do with the beautiful and positive mysticism of the entire process of human life.

The correct Catholic Christian teaching on human sexuality is based on the positive spirituality and mysticism of the sanctity of life and its complete process from natural conception to natural death. It is about the mutual giving and receiving, the proverbial male and female of the creative process, and not artificially impeding the natural processes of creation. It is a sexual manifestation of an entire approach to the life cycles of the environment. While giving priority to human life, this teaching can apply to all life. This has vast ramifications that we are only beginning to realize in our ecological coexistence with the environment. This is much more than simply obeying even a good ideology about sex. It is about the mystical and practical spirituality of love and life.

Married chastity means that you will give your love completely to one special person for the rest of your life. Only in the safety and security of such a commitment can one stand in complete emotional nakedness before another. Next to our intimacy with God, this is the most intimate relationship that can be shared on earth. From that complete self-giving comes new life in the form of children. This is a special sign of the love between Jesus and the church. It is sacramental and holy. Just as the mutual self-giving between Jesus and the church produces spiritual children in the form of converts, so does marriage in the form of actual children. The commitment to stick around and raise them without running off here and there to follow your own fancies and whims is no small thing. It is a great gift of self-emptying love that when practiced correctly gives children a gift that will stay with them for life.

Celibate spirituality is also most powerful. I have lived as a married person and as a celibate. Both states of life are gifts from God. The celibate state of life is a sacrifice to be sure, but it is a sacrifice of love that bears most powerful fruit. There are times of intense loneliness. But this almost forces one to face God because one has no human outlet for deeper intimacy. There are no human relationships to hide behind. Without that outlet, one must either find intimacy with God on a spiritual level or simply dry up as a human being. Sadly, some celibates have done the latter. But many realize the former and go on to great spiritual depths and heights. It has been my experience that celibates either become cranky old people or they retain a perceptible childlikeness that is downright saintly. Celibacy is a radical call for the few who have received it. It tends to produce radical results. Some of these are good, and some are not so good and even plain bad when the gift is received and used badly. But when the results are good, they are very good indeed. Many saints have come forth from those who have embraced this gift from God. That is why celibacy has been held as a special gift from God in the monastic traditions of the world. The new monasticism is no different.

But there is an inner chastity of heart and mind that applies to both celibacy and marriage that goes even deeper. This is about being the chaste spouse of Jesus himself as his bride. The Scriptures say that the church is the bride of Christ. St. Bernard of Clairvaux, St. Bonaventure, St. John of the Cross, and others say that each individual soul is a bride of Christ as well. This is what we call spousal or bride/bridegroom mysticism.

We are all called to this mental and emotional purity. When the pond of our thoughts and emotions is turbulent, it is difficult to see what is in the pond of our soul. When the pond is quiet and still, then we can see what is really going on. When we can see, then we can begin the process of purification. Indeed, the act of simply stilling the waters clears our soul of many turbulent thoughts and feelings. This is accomplished through healthy meditation whereby we still the body and breath so that the emotions and thoughts settle down. Then we can focus the thoughts, which direct the emotions, and the body can become the house for the entire process.

There are two motions in the release of self that make self-giving possible. One is upward in the selfless passion of love for God alone that is most charismatic. The other is contemplative prayer where the old self just falls away like an old set of clothes that no longer fits well. Both methods are powerful ways to let go of the self that is sometimes stuck in unchaste thoughts that stir up unhealthy sexual desires.

A great help in this process is spiritual direction. One of the ancient methods of spiritual direction is the "revelation of thoughts" spoken of by the monastic tradition of the East and the West. This is the core of what is sometimes called "monastic confession."

The Rule of St. Benedict in chapter 4 says, "As soon as wrongful thoughts come into your heart, dash them against Christ and disclose them to your spiritual father [or mother]" (RB 4.50). This is a Western expression of an entire monastic tradition that can be found in the East and the West.

Monastic confession is distinct from sacramental confession. In sacramental confession we only confess our actual sins of omission and commission and of thought and deed. In monastic confession we also confess our temptations as well as our entire thought and emotional patterns. This can only happen voluntarily with a director you really trust and often takes some time to move into. When the director is unfit, this relationship can become abusive, and the church has norms regarding the protection of the individual and the conscience that are wholesome when rightly observed. But once practiced with a trusted and wise director, it is a great treasure in the relationship of director and disciple.

The new monasticism calls all people, celibate, single, and married, to embrace an interior chastity that is a great aid to meditation, prayer, and union with God, and it is expressed and strengthened through human sexuality itself. It is not always easy. But it is most rewarding for those who will dare to embrace the higher calling of interior and exterior chastity in the midst of today's most promiscuous culture. It is a great way to spiritual purity and clarity. It is the higher way of the Universal Monk.

Poverty

We are a people addicted to consumerism. When we were a wealthier nation, it caused an unequal distribution of the world's resources. Now that we are a debtor nation, it has caused us to go deeper and deeper into debt. We are now addicted to a lifestyle we cannot pay for, and we are passing the bills to future generations. China now owns around 20 percent of the national debt of the United States. In real estate and business interests, it owns and controls much, much more. The only reason it does not cash in debt is because we are the ones consuming its products, creating a symbiotic relationship of consuming codependency. We live in an alarming time where our nation is changing into something it has never been before and was never dreamed of by the framers of the Constitution.

But there is a way out. The New Monasticism extends the blessings of an ancient teaching that is the remedy to this vice.

Avarice is the third of the classical eight vices of early eastern monasticism. It is the desire for many possessions. But it can also be applied to the desire to control things, situations, and even other people. It is one of the three leading vices because failure to satisfy its desires leads to anger and sad bitterness that leads to an unhealthy sloth and apathy that causes one to simply give up. This ends in spiritual death.

Jesus teaches that all his followers must renounce every possession, every relationship, and even their very self in order to follow him. The community of the early church in Jerusalem held all things in common. St. Paul says that even though we may retain private ownership, we are to consider all things common and share with the poor so that there is certain equality between rich and poor in the church. These teachings were not for an elite few but for every follower of Jesus and the entire church. But the church has fallen away from these teachings through the centuries, and now we struggle again with consumerism and the unequal distribution of the world's resources as a very real cause for conflict, crime, and war.

The early monks tried to restore the purity of this teaching on gospel simplicity and poverty. The monks of the desert lived in cells that could be constructed in one day with the help of the other monks and grew most of the meager food they consumed. As monasteries developed, private ownership was renounced, and they lived by the work of their hands and the donations of the faithful. The mendicants of the thirteenth century returned to a radical simplicity in imitation of the poverty of Jesus and the apostles who had "nowhere to lay their heads."

The Rule of St. Benedict says in the thirty-third chapter on private ownership, "Above all, this evil practice must be uprooted and removed from the monastery. . . . *All things should be the common possession* of all, as it is written, *so that no one* presumes to *call anything his own* (Acts 4:32)" (RB 33.1, 6).

But it goes on in the next chapter to say:

> It is written, *Distribution was made to each one as he had need* (Acts 4:35). By this we do not imply that there should be favoritism—God forbid—but rather consideration for weaknesses. Whoever needs less should thank God and not be distressed, but whoever needs more should feel humble because of his weakness, not self-important because of the kindness shown him. In this way all the members will be at peace. (RB 34.1-5)

There is a consistent tradition of renunciation with all the monastic traditions of the world. The Hebrew prophets of old often joined in schools of prophets and lived a simple life learning from a teacher. The Essenes held all things in common. The Buddhist bhikshus and Hindu sannyasi renounce all personal possessions. The sages of China live most simply. The Sufis of Islam live a very simple life. When I visited India, I was struck by the complete renunciation that all single and married members of most ashrams make in order just to live there.

Today there is a need to return to a radical but not fanatical gospel simplicity again. In our integrated monastery all celibates renounce private ownership, singles may retain some private possessions, and families may keep a bit more due to the legitimate needs of families with children. In practice most of us work at the monastery, so we hold things in common and simply meet the legitimate needs of all our members of all states of life according to our ability. The entire community tries to live very real gospel simplicity. Our domestic members retain full private ownership but try to live simply and meet the needs of community, the church, and the poor in substantive and appropriately sacrificial ways.

We live in a world where the majority of our world's populations are desperately poor, and the small minority controls most of the world's resources. Such inequalities are the cause of much pain and suffering in our world.

Pope John Paul II said that the few have much and the many have little. The problem is that the more the few who have much get, the more they want and the more essentially unsatisfied they become. As we say, consumerism consumes the consumer. As Jesus said, "Wherever your treasure is, there will you find your heart."

Plus, when the many realize that the few have the little they really need, they will eventually rise up in revolution to get it. Often that revolution is bloody. So, if we want to fulfill

Jesus' teaching that "blessed are the peacemakers," the few who have the much will give to the many who have the little so that their legitimate needs might be met. This will cause everyone to be more satisfied and will help bring peace to the world. But this renunciation by the few must be a voluntary gift of love in response to the voluntary love gift of Jesus if it is to be truly Christian. Otherwise it just brings an oppression of individual liberty.

St. Augustine said that whatever we use that we do not really need, we steal from the needy. In our community we say to differentiate between our wants and our needs because habitually indulging our wants kills the needy. This is really quite a show stopper! We discover that most of the things we use are not really needs but only wants. Such a simple question will find us divesting ourselves of racks of clothes, household items, technological toys, and a lot of "feel good" food! It will radically simplify our life.

But we also teach that God wants to give us some wants. God is a God of love and wants to bless his people. For instance, we may like an occasional dessert. I don't think that God minds it either! Treating a loved one or friend to a little gift every now and then is an act of love that can make life a bit more special.

But if I begin to think that I "need" a daily dessert, then I am becoming addicted to my "want." As we say, if you begin to think that your wants are needs, then you are becoming addicted to your wants. Addiction is usually tragic. In truth, many of us are addicted to our Western consumerism. Renunciation of our wants is a basic monastic and gospel value that can help break us of this addiction to consumerism.

But this peace and justice aspect to gospel poverty or simple living can easily degenerate into something ugly and gray. God wants to give brilliant color to everyone's lives, rich and poor alike! Poverty must be a love response to God, to people, and to all creation. It can never be some gray-faced mathematical equation between the haves and the have-nots.

As we say in our BSC Way of Life:

> Gospel poverty is essentially a love response to God and to people. The beauty of gospel poverty is found in love. Poverty without love is an ugly curse that brings pain and death to the very people created in the image of our life-giving God. On the other hand, love without the sacrifice of poverty is as empty as a lifeless shell. Love is selfless. Selflessness brings sacrifice of self for the sake of others. This sacrifice manifests itself in various expressions of gospel poverty. Gospel poverty cannot be a willing self-sacrifice without love, and love cannot be Christian without the self-sacrifice of poverty. When we become poor in spirit, we come to know the wealth of God's love, and if we know the wealth of God's love, we gladly become poor for the sake of others.

This all has a huge effect on our life of meditation and prayer. If we become addicted, then our senses, emotions, and thoughts will be preoccupied by possessions. We will sit down to meditate and will be completely distracted. Renunciation of these things has been proven by the monastic tradition throughout the ages to provide a better environment for deeper undistracted meditation and prayer. Plus, good meditation and contemplative prayer will also act as an aid to become even more detached from enslavement to external things and addictions.

Again our Way of Life says:

> The Brothers and Sisters of Charity work to be as free as possible from the cares of the world, so that our hearts may be fixed only on heaven. We engage in a life of heavenly prayer, study, and work, free from the cares of this world, which so quickly kills and blinds the spiritual life of freedom. We are bound to as little as possible, so that we may be free to give as

much as possible to anyone who asks when the love of Jesus inspires. We are poor, so that others might be wealthy in the Lord. Motivated by love of God and love of neighbor, we gladly embrace the lowliness of poverty so all might know the exalted glory of true wealth in Jesus.

Jesus says that in order to follow him we must renounce "all our possessions." Not just the ones we aren't using! He gets pretty specific. He says, "If anyone comes to me without hating his father and mother, wife and children, brothers and sisters, and even his own life, he cannot be my disciple." So he mentions three areas: possessions, relationships, and self. Why?

It is not that these things are bad, but that we have used them poorly. Creation is a created gift of God. It is not evil. We need physical things in order to exist in this physical creation.

We need "possessions." The problem is that we are so often possessed by our possessions. Consumerism consumes the consumer. Jesus calls us to renounce our possessions in order to be truly free. Then we can use our possessions to bring God's love into this world.

The same is true of relationships. God has given us relationships and said that it is not good that we live alone. The problem is that we often do relationships poorly. We try to possess others like a possession. This is not love. Love gives to another regardless of what we get back out of the sheer joy of loving another. Manipulation gives in order to get; it loves in order to be loved. That is not love. It is manipulation. Real love finds the greatest reward in loving without expecting reward. Then we gain the greatest reward of all: love itself.

This is also true in understanding of our very self. There is nothing wrong with having a "self." God created us, and we are good. The problem is that we have a self-understanding that is often seriously flawed. We have often allowed ourselves to become a person very different from the person God created us to be. It happens slowly and almost imperceptibly. We mainly do it out of a sense of self-preservation in the midst of a sometimes violent and cruel, fallen world. We put on layer after layer of protection, and before we know it we have become a completely false person. Even our "personality" is not really a reflection of that deepest person God originally created us to be. It is false. As St. Paul says, it is based on "illusion and desire."

When we let go of these things, we discover how they can all be great blessings in our life. When we take up our cross daily and die to these things in Christ, we are resurrected and all these things begin to find their right place in the will of God. We find out who we really are in God. Then all our relationships grow out of who we really are, and we begin to use the things of this world to prosper in our relationships to our family, our church and community, all humanity, and all creation.

The universal new monasticism is a great way to find help in this renunciation process that helps us to prosper spiritually. It helps us to meditate and pray better. It helps us to understand who we really are in God, and it helps us to have better relationships with others and all of creation. It provides a sense of support as we try to live a way that is countercultural to modern society, but ultimately makes us better members of society. It helps to bring us the poverty of Jesus and the greatest wealth we can ever posses.

In our Way of Life we say:

> The ascetical discipline of gospel poverty is like the pruning of the wild growth from a fruit tree. Initially, it seems to cut the tree back to almost nothing, but in the long run it causes the tree to actually become more fruitful. Likewise, with the gospel poverty. Initially, it seems to deprive a person or a community from any earthly pleasure, but in the long run it causes even our earthly life to be more fruitful.
>
> Ultimately, gospel poverty is a naked embrace of the paradox of the cross of Jesus Christ. Gospel poverty must be a love response to God and to people, and the highest expression of

God's love is in the self-emptying of God in the incarnation of Jesus Christ and his death on the cross for the sake of the salvation of the world. Therefore, the logic of poverty is found in love, and the highest expression of love is found in the cross. Therefore, gospel poverty makes ultimate sense only in the light of the cross of our Lord Jesus Christ.

But there is yet another most mystical poverty spoken of by Meister Eckhart. It is a poverty beyond external possessions and ideas, names or forms. It is the complete poverty of contemplative union. It is here that we finally possess the wealth that can only be found through poverty. Eckhart says that after having embraced all the preparatory stages of external poverty and the detachment of poverty of spirit, we must even let go of God in order to fully possess or be possessed by God. He says that we must renounce God in order to find God.

This is not to say that using names for God is not necessary and even good at the stages of spiritual life approaching pure contemplation. There is even a spirituality of the Divine Names in the Christian and non-Christian East whereby the Name embodies the Being of God. So, simply praying the Name brings us into union with the very Being of God.

But names on earth are temporary things. Each of us will be given a new name in heaven that is kept secret from us for now. These "names" reflect an inner reality of who we really are that is beyond any earthly name. Jesus' name is above every other name. But on earth it is pronounced differently in different languages. His name is really beyond any human name. It is a reality beyond what we can know with our mind here on earth. It can only be intuited with our spirit in his Spirit. It is a Name beyond all names.

So in addition to the positive way of cataphatic affirmation, there is the way of apophatic negation. Since God is beyond limit, we can actually say more about what we know of God by saying what we do not know. We find his greatest action in sacred stillness and his Being by letting go of being. This is called the way of "unknowing," or "divine darkness," in Christian tradition.

God is beyond names and forms in his pure Being. He simply *is*. He Exists. This is why the letters YHWH are used in Hebrew texts to speak of God in his purity beyond names or what we can say with our lips. The names of God are all emanations that allow us to know aspects of the *one*. As soon as we give God the name "god," then he is no longer fully God because we have limited him to a name and form. He is beyond such dualities. He simply *is*. We are the ones who have fallen into the world of this and that, I and thou, and being and nonbeing. Before the Fall, it was not so. There was no good or evil. Everything simply existed in the One Who Exists. Only after breaking union with him did we find ourselves in a world of dualistic separation. Since that time God has reached into this dualistic world through his emanations in order to bring us back to pure Being.

But we should end with a word of caution. The notion of finding God by renouncing God is profound but should only be embraced by those who have first followed God through his Name and emanations into creation through the positive things of spirituality and religion. To think ourselves ready for pure contemplative Being before we have been adequately prepared through positive faith and morality is a recipe for frustration and despair. Without the outward forms of religion, we can all too easily end up wandering through the desert of aimless and misguided spirituality that leads to the great abyss of unhealthy nothingness. This is not the end result of the true apophatic way of pure contemplation.

So I invite you to embrace the complete poverty of Jesus Christ. It will make both your external and internal life better. It will simplify your life and make all things clear in a cloudy and muddy world. It will also prepare the way for the greatest poverty of all. Completely let go of all things through the cross of Christ, including your very self, so that you might find the resurrected All within yourself through the power of the Holy Spirit. Then you will find God beyond God and the One Who Exists with your very existence. Then you will be resurrected, born again, and restored to the original grace of being a pure child of God.

Conversion of Life

"Repent, for the kingdom of God is at hand!" This was the first "sermon" that Jesus ever preached. It was also the message of John the Baptist. We have heard it from fiery-eyed evangelists on TV and on street corners. It is often a message of the condemnation and judgment of an angry God that fills us with guilt rather than love. For those it converts, it often turns them into angry and judgmental people as well. For most of us it has become a turnoff to religion and God.

But real repentance is something quite different, and most essential to any disciple who follows the master of any spiritual way or religion. Jesus is no exception.

Real repentance is the call of a loving God who wants our lives to be abundant and full. We have often gotten sidetracked into lifestyle currents that do not really work. They bring us pain and suffering. They fill our lives with frustration, anger, and bitterness. They program us to negativity rather than the positive and wonderful things of life. God really does want to "save" us from such things because he really does love us.

"Repentance" simply means to "turn around." It is where we get the word "penance." The Greek word is *metanoia*. It means conversion. It involves an act of the will and interior contrition that prompt us to turn away from the things in our life that are hurtful and cause suffering and nonredemptive pain, or what we call sin.

St. Benedict uses a similar language in describing the commitments a monk makes when he becomes a member of a monastery. In chapter 58 of the Rule of St. Benedict, "The Procedure For Receiving Brothers," it says, "When he is to be received, he comes before the whole community in the oratory and promises stability, fidelity to monastic life, and obedience" (RB 58.17). "Fidelity to monastic life" has often been translated as "conversion of life" or "conversion of manners." The word actually used in the text is *conversatio*. It is difficult to translate, and no English translation fully captures the original meaning.

The most essential meaning is simply conversion or repentance. As noted above, this simply means to turn around. This conversion has come from two motivations. The first is attrition. The second is contrition. Attrition means a conversion based on common sense. We can see that the direction our life has been headed leads to sorrow and pain. As Scripture says, "The wages of sin is death," and, "When sin reaches maturity it begets death." Attrition motivates us through simple self-preservation based on a more eternal perspective of reality.

Contrition goes much deeper. It includes a sorrow for sin that is based on the relational aspect of our life with a loving God. We realize that God is personal and that he really loves us. When we sin, it breaks that relationship. Some have said that it "hurts" God. (In Scripture God is given human emotions of compassion, love, and even anger.) Who of us has not been hurt when our love is betrayed by someone we have loved to the point of mingling our lives with theirs in a significant way? At the very least, when we realize this genuine love relationship, it causes us a godly sorrow for the sin we have committed and great gratitude for the forgiveness offered when we turn back toward God.

When combined with monastic stillness and silence, we see the essence of this and are extremely grateful for the forgiveness God gives to one who turns back. There is a story of an old monk on Mount Athos that all he does is walk around and ask everyone, "What do you think, are we being saved today?" As he asks this, he gently weeps holy tears of sorrow and joy. Nothing more need be said.

I must admit a gradual growth in my personal appreciation of this. When I first turned back to God in the Jesus Movement, it was really more out of attrition than anything else. It just made good sense to turn from the rock 'n roll life to something more positive. I might even say that there was a bit of pride in it. I mean, after all, wouldn't I do the right thing? There was still a lot of arrogance in it.

But then my life began to unravel. Where once my conversion brought me into a better place and all my friends and relatives thought it a very good thing, soon I became a Scripture-quoting Bible thumper. Folks slowly began to back away. I was arrogant and proud. If you had a problem, I had a Scripture! I was always right—or at least I was convinced that I was. But it was a sham. Instead of Jesus' divine incarnation among us humans making me more human through the divine gift, I was simply becoming less human. This is never the goal of real religion. But it was not Jesus' fault. I had yet to really repent and change to a healthy spirituality that *he* offered. Most of us have met people like this in religious life. They aren't usually much fun to be around!

At that point I began to lose everything, my family, my friends, and finally my job. I grew organic vegetables and sold them door-to-door. There was nothing in my future. Instead of my spirituality attracting people, it often pushed them away. I was lost, despite my claiming to be saved by Jesus, the Savior. After a while I began to realize my error. When there were very few people left close to me, I was finally brought to my knees. I could only turn to God and the example of the great saints. I was broken. I was ready for the deeper conversion.

It was at that point in my life that I experienced some contrition. I stumbled into a Franciscan retreat center in Indianapolis, and the kindly friars took me in. They never pressured me to become a Catholic or join the Franciscans. They simply gave me a place to stay and made me feel at home. They joked with me, poked fun at me with brotherly affection. They offered me a space and time to heal by loving me in the real Jesus. I walked the wooded grounds and cried a lot. Slowly I began to heal. My present vocation was born out of that experience and remains essential to my life today.

But that was not the end. Since then I have gone through a continual cycle of attrition and contrition. My relationship with Jesus can get pretty dry and even legalistic at times. I have made many, many mistakes even after that initial conversion of contrition. I can become very "religious" and give in to religious pride that causes me to become rather judgmental. I often found myself focusing too much on Francis, Franciscanism, or monasticism and the church more than on Jesus, who was the purpose of them all. Sometimes it was obvious, and sometimes it was only internal. But it was real. Today, none of this is extreme. Others may not even see it. But it is there. When I retire into solitude and silence, all the masks drop away, and there it is, staring me in the face again. At that point God almost always does some little, or not so little, something to humble me. It is a wake up call, and it brings me back to my senses. It brings me back to my knees. Then I break through to a contrition that cleanses my soul.

In recent years I have been allowed by the community to spend greater time in religious reclusion. This is a tradition not always well understood in the West but has always been a part of the monastic East. At first three and now five days a week I spend in my cell. I pray the Divine Office and eat my meals there. I join the community a few times a week for common prayer, Eucharist, meals, and meetings. The rest of the time I am alone in my cell.

Many people think that I must be breaking through to some kind of esoteric knowledge about God. It isn't true. But I have gotten to know myself pretty well. In solitude there is nothing to hide behind. You are naked before God, alone with the Alone. You are *monos*. You are a monk. The illusions fall away. Suddenly it is the simple things that ring true and become most profound. The simple prayers and Scriptures are often the ones that speak to me the most. The Divine Office has come to have a whole new life and is a great springboard for contemplation. I find that I participate with a new awareness that can usually reduce me to tears at any given moment. Simple conversion overwhelms me through all these things.

In this state I came to a kind of walking repentance. You meditate on the simplest aspect of Jesus and the church and find the gift of contrition and compunction right there in the midst of it. You break through to tears. It stops being a single experience and becomes a state of mind. It becomes a way of life. This does not disable you. It sets you free. This deep compunction actually brings you greater joy as you begin to savor each moment and every relationship. You break through to eternity in every moment and find every moment made richer in the eternal now.

This is what *conversatio* is really about. It is a walking, ongoing state of conversion. It is a kind of walking meditation. It is a conversion of "life." It is a way of life. That is why the Rule of Benedict calls it "conversion of life."

But I could not have entered into this kind of solitude without having first been trained through community life. They were inseparable. Only the disciplines I learned in community made my life in solitude something other than an exercise in self-indulgence in the name of God and a meandering without structure through a land of illusion in a kind of spiritual anarchy. Going daily to common prayer made the Liturgy of the Hours a discipline that became second nature for me, and I committed most of the psalms to memory. Daily common meals made eating something done for God and for fellowship with others, not just about satisfying my stomach and tastes. These communal disciplines prepared me for greater solitude so that solitude would not become a place where I wandered off into illusions and darkness. Monastic community prepared me for monastic solitude. The two are inseparable.

So the conversion of life in the Rule of Benedict is always in the context of life in community. As Christian hermits are always seen in the context of the people of God, so the monastic hermit is always seen in the context of the monastic community. The vow is not just personal. It is personal within the context of the community.

It is also ongoing. Conversion is to a way of life for the remainder of your life. It is not once and for all. It is daily. That is why Catholics and monks speak of "daily conversion." Since we are in a relationship, every day we wake up and make a decision to grow in that relationship or not. Before the profession of stability, conversion of life, and obedience, or before the evangelical counsels in other communities, the candidate is asked, "What do you seek?" With conversion of life we ask ourselves that question every day. That simple question keeps all things in the right priority of importance and keeps our monastic life on course. It is daily. And it is serious. But it also leads to great freedom and joy. Every day becomes a point of further conversion to God through Jesus.

This is brought out in a powerful way by the original word, *conversatio*. This conversion is not static. It is a living relationship with God in community that involves "conversation." It is an ongoing dialogue between God, the soul, the individual, and the community. It is a complete whole where one really cannot be understood fully without the other. It is a conversional trinity of sorts.

I am reminded of Francis and the first friars. When people would see them, they would ask which community they belonged to. They certainly did not say that they were "the first Franciscans!" They did not even say, "Friars Minor," for they were not yet an official community in the church. They responded only that they were "penitents from Assisi." They were people ready to turn around radically from their past life that had not brought them spiritual rebirth. They had been, and were being, spiritually born again in the Spirit of Jesus.

Most of us are pretty much like those first Franciscans. We may or may not be a part of a formal community. But we are ready for a change. We are ready to repent and enter into a conversion of life that will change our life for the better. Like the Benedictine commitment to conversion of life, we usually want to find some support group or community within which to make that change so that we will stick with it when we grow weary and want to give up. But there is something much deeper than one single community at work here. It is a Universal Monasticism that calls deep within our heart that cannot be denied or fully described. That is the call of the New Monasticism. But to enter this community, we have to fully repent, let go of the old self, and follow the way of the way, truth, and life taught by Jesus. We must profess conversion of life. I pray that you all respond to the call and begin a life of daily conversion within this ancient and ever-new community.

Stability

We live in a very unstable world today. There is a huge shift going on globally. China owns a portion of the United States but is dependent on our trade dollars for its continued prosperity. India's population and education are growing and are close to surpassing that of China. The rise of fundamentalist and extremist Islam is of great concern for those seeking peace based on unity in the diversity of religious and political expressions around the world. The United States is struggling with the tensions between larger or smaller federal government as it integrates into the larger global approach to governance. The pros and cons of bailouts, stimulus packages under any name, and federalizing health care also affect our national debt and its impact on our economy.

We see this instability in very personal ways. People move from job to job very quickly. Even in prosperity, Americans in the United States moved locations on average once every four or five years. Vocations to marriage or religious celibacy are also in flux. Only about 50 percent of marriages make it. Most children I play for in Catholic schools are from broken homes. The social and psychological effect of this on the next generation is still in question.

Monastic stability speaks to this secular instability. Benedictine monastics actually take a vow of stability. It basically means that monks promise to remain a part of a specific monastery for life. They may be assigned to various ministries and even be part of new monasteries, called "daughter houses," founded from the monastery they promise stability to. But their promise of stability remains intact.

In the selection we quoted before, there is also a reference to stability. In chapter 58 the Rule of St. Benedict says, "When he is to be received, he comes before the whole community in the oratory and promises stability, fidelity to monastic life, and obedience" (RB 58.17).

The prologue says that choosing this way of life is for life, and that when done in love, not law, it is not burdensome but rather life-giving:

> But as we progress in this way of life and in faith, we shall run on the path of God's commandments, our hearts overflowing with inexpressible delight of love. Never swerving from his instructions, then, but faithfully observing his teaching in the monastery until death, we shall through patience share in the sufferings of Christ that we may deserve also to share in his kingdom. Amen. (RB Prol. 49-50)

As we have seen, this is in contrast to so-called monks who live on their own, not under an abbot, and tend to move from place to place. They are called "gyrovagues." The RB says:

> Fourth and finally, there are the monks called gyrovagues, who spend their entire lives drifting from region to region, staying as guests for three or four days in different monasteries. Always on the move, they never settle down, and are slaves to their own wills and gross appetites. (RB 1.10-11)

But the early monastic tradition was not so clear and not so rigid. When St. Antony felt that his hermitage was too open to the intrusion of visiting monks and disciples, he moved to his inner mountain. St. John Cassian went to Bethlehem and joined the monastic community there. But he moved on to Egypt in order to go to the source of the monastic movement. While those in Bethlehem frowned on this, had he not followed this inspiration we would never have received his famous *Institutes* and *Conferences* that so shaped all monastic expressions in Europe. The Rule of St. Benedict, which became so definitive in Western monasticism, was deeply shaped by Cassian. As we shall see, St. Benedict developed his rule as the Roman Empire was breaking apart, and the need for greater stability was needed against the instability of the secular world of that time.

We used to have a saying in our community that we had to "find the stability of instability." In other words, we find an inner stability that transcends the outer instability of our modern world. Especially in our culture, we see person after person come and go from our community. Those who stay must find an inner stability to persevere.

Most of the Benedictine monks we think about lived in a culture where people moved around very little. The average person would likely never travel much farther from home than a neighboring village or two. Only the lords of a region would travel from one region to another to engage in business between regions and states. Only they had the opportunity to travel more like we do today.

This was called the feudal system. After the fall of the Roman Empire, barbarian tribes reigned with violence and terror across Europe. It was the feudal system that established some stability. Essentially, lords were established over a region. These lords owned the lands and controlled everything within their domain. This included agriculture and specialty trades in the villages. Each individual in the realm actually belonged to the lords and paid taxes to them. In exchange, the lords were to benevolently provide for the basic needs of the people.

In that feudalistic system, monasticism was established by gifts from kings and princes, who gave them land and built monasteries for the monks to live in. They were given feudal lands, and their abbots were established as local lords, paying their daily expenses by collecting taxes from the people of the region who lived on abbey lands under their care. This was how the monasteries could function in this system. It was this arrangement that allowed monasticism to spread across Europe at that time. And monasteries prospered in a way never before dreamed possible.

Because of this the average monk, much like the average person, would rarely have a need to leave the monastery. He would live, pray, and work within the monastery of their profession. Only the leaders of a monastery would really need to travel to other monasteries or local areas.

But this rather ideal system was only as good as the lords who oversaw it. As soon as lords, bishops, and abbots began to be overly selfish and greedy, the system began to work against the very people it was meant to protect. Uprisings began against the feudal system, where average people began to take back power from greedy lords. A democracy of sorts was being born.

At the same time there was a move away from the traditional barter system where the average person simply traded goods, and only lords traded with money in a substantive way. As average people gained more power, they began to engage in business trade. This meant that they also began to travel. So, businesspeople began to move around the world in order to buy and sell in connection with their business. A new capitalism was being born.

All of this meant that average folks began to travel from place to place more frequently. Europe and the whole Western world were on the move. The old stability of feudalism was disappearing and would soon be gone.

One such city where this occurred was Assisi in Italy. The townsfolk rose up in the last years of the twelfth century and overthrew the local lord, defeating the local lord's army and tearing down the castle, the Rocca Maggiore, with farm tools and their bare hands. The pope sided with the townsfolk, for he recognized that the old system was corrupt and was on its way out.

St. Francis of Assisi was a son of this reform and represented a religious expression of this new cultural movement. Many groups were part of this religious movement. Many went too far in their protests against the corruption of the old feudal church and lapsed into schism and heresy. But Francis is an example of one who made this same religious movement without going too far into heterodoxy. He remained a true son of the orthodox Catholic Church. This is what made him different. This is what made him so popular. This is what made him a saint.

Francis gave birth to a new monasticism in his day. What made it most unique was its universality. He basically changed the scope of the monastery cloister to include the entire world! As he said, "The world is my cloister, my body is my cell, and my soul is the hermit within." This was nothing short of revolutionary. All of the mendicant orders like the Carmelites, the Augustinians, the Dominicans, and many more, soon followed this example.

This came very close to the gyrovagues and sarabaites that the Rule of St. Benedict had cautioned against. They did, indeed, move from house to house around the world. But they did not do so without being under obedience to a rule and a superior. This is what made all the difference. They had a central leader over the entire community, and each region was organized into provinces with local houses. Friars could be assigned by obedience from house to house and from region to region. Had they simply wandered at will, they would have justly fallen under the condemnation of the established monastic tradition. As it was, they became a new monasticism that brought life to the old as well.

From then on, all communities would have a sense of centralization under a general superior. Even the more monastic-based Benedictines developed a central facilitator called the abbot primate, or the "first abbot." In the more active communities it was now possible to be assigned to many local houses in the course of one's lifetime while remaining a member of one international community. While the more traditional monastic communities would retain a commitment to stability to their home monastery, a greater sense of being one international movement would develop, and entire new communities made up of members from various monasteries would even become possible.

Today we are also facing major cultural shifts and changes. The new monasticism of today addresses them and accommodates them. Most new communities include the possibility to live in many different local monastic houses in the course of one's lifetime. But there is really more. Today the integrations of various spiritualities and states of life give a more broad perspective to the entire community. These seeming opposites might have seemed "unstable" in times past, but today the broadness of this base actually makes a community more stable.

These areas are the integrations we mentioned earlier. Contemplative and charismatic, spontaneous and liturgical, contemplative base and apostolic action with the new evangelization, and celibate, single, and family vocations are now equal parts of one community with different expressions rather than autonomous communities in one spiritual family. This is nothing short of revolutionary in today's environment.

Today's great challenge remains reestablishing stability in one community in the midst of the disintegration of every vocation in modern culture. This is a double challenge. It is interior and exterior. It means finding the inner "stability of instability," and establishing real external vocational stability in the midst of our highly unstable world. It is just as relevant today as it was in the time of St. Benedict or St. Francis. Though the particulars of expression may adapt and change, monastic stability remains a witness to Jesus, who remains the same, "yesterday, today, and forever."

But all in the world is not bad news. Joel Kotkin's groundbreaking book about America as we move toward 2050, *The Next Hundred Million: America in 2050*, reports a shift from the destabilization of previous generations toward greater stability. He says that people are getting married later but staying together longer, some for life. People are having more children. That represents a new optimism about the future, even while facing the pessimistic challenges of contemporary society. There is a growing trend toward active spirituality, even though many people turn away from the formal religion of their upbringing and organized religion in general. Folks are opting to stay in local areas instead of moving around every few years. They are even turning down job offers in order to stay in a local area and build up a local community. All these things are signs of hope regarding greater stability in our society after a time of some of the greatest instability in our history.

There is a Universal Monasticism on the rise. The New Monasticism is giving expression to it. It brings stability to a still unstable world. We have the obligation to help bring us back from the brink of societal destabilization and to help encourage the beginning signs of greater stability on every level of life. This makes for healthier individuals and, in turn, makes for a better world.

New Members

Folks always get excited about the next new thing. I remember a Vince Gill song about the "Next Big Thing" in country music. It is also true of Christian music and of traveling ministries in general. It is also true of movements in the church. We have already addressed this regarding seekers when considering Benedict's treatment of gyrovagues. But it is also true even of those who seek to join a monastery. Many say that they want to join a monastery, but when the going gets tough (and it will hit everyone sooner or later), many choose to leave in search of something else. The old saying, "When the going gets tough, the tough get going," has sometimes been misinterpreted to mean that when things get difficult, take off and go somewhere else! Often we find that despite a lot of talking about a lifetime commitment and the need for stability in a constantly changing world, many folks just cannot stay in one place for long. That is why a quality period of time for discernment is so necessary in today's culture.

The Rule of St. Benedict goes to some length to describe the one-year period designed to test whether one is really suited for monastic life. It allows for a person to leave at various times during that trial period. It says that they must first stay in the guesthouse. Then if they are really serious, they may be received into the monastery novitiate for new members. They are placed under an older monk who is supposed to explain the life and prepare them for a lifetime commitment. During that time they are to have the entire rule read to them so that they will fully understand what they are making a commitment to.

This was not always the case. In the beginning of monasticism, you simply went into the desert, placed yourself under an elder spiritual father, and were clothed in the monastic habit. That was it! After that you were expected to learn from the spiritual father and imitate his life and prayer. There were no specific formal vows that we know of. But to depart after becoming a monk was considered a shameful thing to do. Some church councils even call this "apostasy"! But apparently this did not work out so well. Eventually we hear of the trial period that is now called the "novitiate." The novitiate is sometimes a specific place in monasteries where novices live. A novice is simply a new member who is temporarily testing and being tested in the monastic life.

This pattern was also seen with the first Franciscans. There were friars living in this radical new gospel community, calling people to give up everything and follow Jesus. Thousands responded! At first they simply renounced the world, put on the Franciscan habit, and followed the preacher. But soon real problems emerged as some proved unprepared and unsuited for such a radical gospel life. We do not know exactly how many, but enough departed that the church required the Franciscans to institute a formal novitiate and to limit the power to receive new members to the major superior of each region and province.

This has pretty much proven to be the pattern ever since with all new religious communities in the church. Today we use an even greater screening process and more complete formation program. In our community we start with a rather significant screening process and have a graduated process of entry into full membership.

First an individual comes as a candidate for a two-week period or so. During that time they live with the community and share in most aspects of the way of life. They also meet with leaders who talk to them about their vocation. They must be in good health, finished with their desired level of education, debt free, and living a chaste Catholic and/or Christian life for at least two or more years. They also take a psychological evaluation to indicate if they suffer from any serious emotional or psychological problems that might prove problematic in the future. If all this looks good, they are invited to return for the postulancy.

The postulancy is a six- to twelve-month period in which one lives the life without becoming a member. It is a time to "postulate," or pose a question. They question or discern their vocation, and the community questions it as well. Either have the right to disengage at any time. If the postulancy is completed successfully, then they are invited to enter the novitiate.

The novitiate is a one- to two-year period where a person becomes a member but not one with full rights. It is a time of further preparation, training, and testing. While not allowed to study theology and such, they are educated in the history and spirituality of monasticism and of the community they are joining. It is not a scholastic study, but it is rather complete. They can leave or be asked to leave at any time, even though most are encouraged to complete the testing period before making a decision. It is mutually discerned between the new member and the community as to whether or not one should advance to the next stage of temporary profession.

Temporary profession is the first time the monk will profess the vows of poverty, chastity, and obedience. Benedictines profess stability and an ongoing conversion of life, *conversatio*, and the evangelical counsels are implied. Other communities may pronounce other vows as well. But all these professions are temporary. During this period the new member goes through continuing education. It is in this time that most communities allow some to go forward for training for clerical ordination or further training for lay ministry and such. This is a three-year period that may be repeated once and even twice under extraordinary circumstances. The member may depart or be dismissed in this period but only for a serious reason and after a year or so of discernment. If all goes well, one is finally received into a permanent profession in which one becomes a member with full rights and obligations.

This is no small process. It can take anywhere from four to nine years! It can be likened to an intensive and long engagement between a potential husband and wife. But, we figure that we should really discern a decision as important as this.

Even with all of this in place, the departure rate of members is still rather astonishing in today's culture. Communities tend to be houses with a revolving door. As soon as some come in, some go out! We live in a highly transient and unstable culture. People carry all kinds of baggage from broken families and other relationships. Plus, the culture itself encourages folks to seek newer horizons and relationships almost constantly. So, modern folks tend to come and go a lot. Consequently, the stable social structures of families and even monasteries are threatened. To think that this does not also prevail in monasteries made up of people from this culture is to live in a denial that will eventually lead to intense frustration. Only the monastery that comes to grips with this dynamic will prevail with any semblance of inner or external peace.

A similar process applies to leaving a monastic community. We figure that you should put as much energy into discerning departure as you do for entry. But in actual practice this sometimes proves unrealistic, and dispensation from profession is granted earlier. This is pretty much the pattern used by most celibate communities in the Roman Catholic Church today. It may vary from community to community, but the basic process is consistent throughout.

But there is another aspect to many new monastic communities. Many of these new communities include families as well as celibates. Some include Catholics and non-Catholic Christians. Some, but not many, even include non-Christians in some capacity. This all makes for a more complex and sometimes complicated discernment process, though the actual stages remain the same.

With celibates you only have to discern one individual. With families you have to discern seriously as a couple. You also have to discern if the children are truly happy with this way of life. This considerably compounds, and sometimes complicates, the discernment of new members. Often only one spouse really, really wants to come, and the other is just being supportive. We have found that this rarely works out. Sooner or later the "supportive" spouse will simply find a life as demanding as this unbearable. The couple will have to leave for the sake of their marriage.

The same is true with kids. If one or more of the children do not want to come, it will become very difficult for them, and they will make the entire family miserable. We have found that this is especially true when families bring older children here. In a sense they ask, "What happened to mom and dad?" A few years ago they were living a rather normal American lifestyle. Now they have gotten too radical and just downright weird! It is almost impossible for a child at this stage to adjust unless he or she also really "gets it" and really wants it as well. Parents cannot let the tail wag the dog, but some realistic and fair accommodation has to be made for the development of the child. Because of this, we recommend that families come either at the beginning of their child-raising stage or wait until after the nest has been emptied.

The Hindus have considered this and come up with some wisdom that is helpful, though we cannot apply it uncritically. They recognize four stages of life. The first is the student, where one is trained in a monastic setting under a guru. The second is the householder, where one gets married, gets a good job, and raises a family. The third, is the forest dweller, where a husband and wife go alone or together into the forest to devote themselves entirely to religion and spirituality. The fourth is the sannyasi, or renouncer, where one gives up absolutely everything and wanders on foot alone in complete union with God beyond all names or forms.

We have found that the third stage applies to many who are entering retirement after their children are grown. They often want to give themselves more intensely to their spiritual lives and find a place like an integrated monastery as a good setting for such a thing. The rub in our culture is that many grandparents are expected or want to spend great amounts of time with their grandchildren, so that real involvement in an integrated monastic community life with any real responsibility becomes most difficult.

The second stage applies to parents just starting out. Most kids begin with a strong attachment to their mothers. Then they move into the first stage where greater religious training is possible and desirable. An integrated monastery provides a great setting where children can get that monastic training without actually having to leave home.

The Anabaptist tradition also provides a great example of something similar. More intentionally constituted communities like the Bruderhof, the Hutterites, Amish, Old Order Mennonites, and early Quakers all point to quasi-monastic communities that include children. This is usually successful, though not without criticism. Many children leave these communities in more rebellious years. But the vast majority of them freely choose to return and become full adult members. We could certainly use some of that in modern Western culture.

Most modern monastic and integrated monastic communities have also stumbled onto a solution for the built-in Western societal transience: monastic volunteers. Monasteries are finding that since many want to live in a monastery temporarily, why not provide an intentional way for folks to do just that? Some call it a monastic experience.

At Little Portion we have done both. We receive some who retain a rather secular identity. Others want to adopt a monastic identity more fully for a temporary period of time, so we give them a hooded tunic shirt to wear at community prayers and other functions. It makes them feel "clothed" in the monastic experience for a while. We have taken all kinds of good people who want to come live with us for a period of weeks or months. Some even stay for years. But it is with the understanding that they might choose to leave, so we do not put them in any vital positions of responsibility. Nonetheless, they become active and welcomed participants in our way of life.

Our domestic expression is far less structured, and some just come to our domestic cell groups without joining. For members, we have all the same stages of discernment but with an understanding that they are called to live in the secular world and attend a local parish. Since the life is less externally intensive in its communal requirements, fewer leave. But some still do. Some find the same challenges to their deeply ingrained old habit patterns simply through the community teachings and association with others who are committed to living out those teachings in secular society. On the other hand, others find it too easy, and it becomes just another church organization, so they also drop out.

New monasteries today have found it wise simply to adopt this tried-and-true model for new members. Some have tried to receive folks more immediately, but it often ends with the same disastrous results of the early monks and friars of centuries ago. Due to the smallness of some of these new communities, this can be a bit of a balancing act as a few people take on a lot of duties. Sometimes even novices take on important jobs. But the institution of the novitiate is still a wise model for new monastics to follow.

The Universal Monk may or may not join a community of like-minded folks, but we recommend it. It has a way of fleshing out the "monastic" ideas you have and testing whether or not they are authentic. Community tests whether you might not be fooling yourself. So your calling to community must be wisely discerned and entered into gradually. You may be called to community but not to a particular expression of it. You may be called for life or only for a period of time. You may be called to live in an actual monastery or to associate with a monastery as a domestic, oblate, or secular.

All of this is OK. But it is important that you not use any of it as an excuse for not completely dying to your old self and allowing yourself to be born again as a new creation. This happens most completely in Christ. Jesus says that we must renounce our possessions, our relationships, and even our very self to follow him. Whatever form of community you choose, it must be a way that provides you with a way to do that. Otherwise, it is just a spiritual game.

Conflicts and Community

So we have given our life to Jesus, renounced everything, and followed him. We do this joyfully and willingly because he is so loving and lovable. We often even join some form of community for mutual support. But then we begin to realize that we often do not get along well with those who have done the same thing. We start to look around at everyone else who has also followed him and ask ourselves, "Who the heck are all these people?" Some of them are OK enough, and some we really like. After all, they have given their lives to follow Jesus too. But there are some whom we would not choose to hang out with in the secular world. Some of them are opinionated, overbearing, and downright weird. They are often hard to get along with. And some seem just a touch crazy! This often creates conflict. But Jesus didn't call us to follow him by ourselves. He said that we must do so with others in community so that our love might be tested as to its authenticity. There's the rub. How do we handle it?

It's really easy to find the solution by blaming others. We live in the era of blame. We love to blame others for the problems of the world. We hear about it on the news all the time, and it is getting worse as news comes to us unfiltered through the sometimes very raw media of blogs and such.

We tend to hold others to almost impossible levels of perfection and then turn on them when they do not live up to our expectations. But, we do not apply the same expectations to ourselves. We are filled with excuses and rationalizations for why such things do not apply to us, but we are all too ready to judge and attack others. We want strict rules with everyone else, but we want to be excused from the rules when it comes to us and our situation. While this is particularly problematic in our time, there has never been a time when this human tendency did not exist. It is nothing new.

Jesus said that we must remove the beam of wood from our own eye first. Then we can see the splinter in our brother or sister's eye and help him or her remove it. Otherwise, we might do them great harm and perhaps even cause them to be blinded by our clumsy attempts. He also said that we are not to judge others. God knows the hearts of others far better than we do!

The monks of almost all the great traditions of the world have addressed this situation. Their answer is simple but radical. They all say to focus first on correcting ourselves, and then maybe we can see clearly to correct others.

The Secular World

Most of us get along with others reasonably well in the modern professional world. It is at home with our families where we tend to have problems. Out in the work world you must get along with others reasonably well or you lose your job. You learn to focus on simply getting the job done with the team, regardless of whether you like everyone on it. Plus, you only have to be with them during work hours. After work we go home where we can pretty much do and say what we want.

The same thing is true at the average church. We only go to church once a week or so. We put on our best "Sunday face," like we put on the proverbial "meeting clothes." But underneath there may be someone else. Even daily communicants in Catholic churches only have to see one another long enough to go to Mass. It is pretty easy to hide who we really are behind the liturgical rites and rituals. The same thing is even true of less intensive expressions of the New Monasticism where geographical community is not required, so we only see one another from time to time throughout the week, month, or year. It is pretty easy to fake good for these times. No one sees us when we go home and live with those who see us daily at our weakest moments when there is no social structure to hide behind.

But the rub is that American families are highly dysfunctional and tend not to stay together long. As James Taylor says in one of his songs, "I was raised up family. Man, I'm glad I'm on my own!" Most families in America are broken. Most children are children of divorce. That trend is slowly starting to change, but it hasn't changed much yet. The sociological effects of this remain to be fully seen.

Monastic communities are much like families, but families with a family business. Like in the professional workplace, we work together in various ministries that must also have a business wing. But unlike the workplace, we also eat together, pray together, recreate together, and sleep in the same buildings or monastic complexes. In short, we rarely get away from one another! In this, the monastic community is more like a large family and carries all the advantages and disadvantages of being so.

In the workplace in the typical American city, if someone does not do their job, you simply let him or her go. If you do not like one job, you find another. After that you will rarely see the folks you once worked with, unless you work in a small specialized field like music or publishing. A monastic community is not like that. In a monastic community you simply have little choice but to work things out if you are going to have a healthy community.

Relationship or Coexistence?

When monks and sisters do not work relationships out, they simply learn to tolerate one another. Often the community then slowly degenerates into a general complacency as a kind of relational and emotional haze descends into every aspect of the community's life. You desperately need new people to join in order to get some fresh spirits into the mix. But no one in his or her right mind wants to join such a community. It has become sick, and he or she doesn't want to catch it! Why would he or she join a community he or she does not enjoy or like?

Then many grow disheartened and start to leave. Even under good circumstances many folks come and go through monasteries nowadays. Very few actually stay for life. Often the best and the brightest depart to go to work in a successful workplace, and the ones who are not so good in the workplace stay because they have nowhere to go. This creates all kinds of relational problems in community. It leaves those who stay with questions like who to trust when so many leave. We think that we are building lifelong relationships, but most are gone within a matter of a few years. This leaves a community of very broken people trying to make a go of a life they want to live but find most difficult to actually make work. Even under good circumstances, it is very difficult to work these things through. It is more difficult when there have been conflict and hurt feelings.

So conflicts must be healthfully resolved in community if community is going to be a healthy experience for those in it. How do we do that?

The most basic way is through the relinquishment of ego-driven self-will through obedience to superiors and all the members. This is a very practical way to live out the cross and resurrection of Jesus. We die to the old self and rise to a whole new way of living through the practical things of daily life. There are also further very practical steps in conflict resolution based on that relinquishment of self-will and helping us to grow in it.

Monastic Confession

In monastic tradition the first step in fleshing this out is often in monastic confession. Monastic confession in the Rule of St. Benedict is a Western continuation of an earlier monastic practice that dates back to the desert and continues today in Eastern monasticism. But as we said earlier, there is a difference between monastic confession and sacramental confession. Monastic confession includes not only sin but also the interior stirrings of the soul even during the temptation to sin. Plus, monastic confession can be made to any spiritual father, mother, or elder, regardless of whether one is a lay monk or a priest. Sacramental confession includes only actual sins of omission or commission and is made to an ordained priest. Sacramental confession developed only after monastic confession met with such success within the monasteries of the East and the West and was a sacramental application of the same thing for the laity in secular parishes.

St. Benedict speaks of dashing your thoughts against the stone by confessing to a spiritual father. In chapter 4, "The Tools for Good Works," it says, "As soon as wrongful thoughts come into your heart, dash them against Christ and disclose them to your spiritual father" (RB 4.50). And in chapter 7 on humility, it says, "The fifth step of humility is that a man does not conceal from his abbot any sinful thoughts entering his heart, or any wrongs committed in secret, but rather confesses them humbly" (RB 7.44). This is a powerful monastic tool that is most ancient.

But this confession is not just vertical to one's superiors. It is also horizontal to all the brothers of the monastery. In chapter 44 of the Rule of St. Benedict, "Satisfaction by the Excommunicated," it says, "Anyone excommunicated for serious faults from the oratory and from the table is to prostrate himself in silence at the oratory entrance at the end of the celebration of the Work of God. He should lie face down at the feet of all as they leave the oratory, and let him do this until the abbot judges he has made satisfaction. Next, at the bidding of the abbot, he is to prostrate himself at the abbot's feet, then at the feet of all that they may pray for him" (RB 44.1-4). He goes on to give further details for this and other less serious faults. The chapter concludes by saying, "They do so until he gives his blessing and says: 'Enough'" (v. 10). After that, he is to be treated equally as all brothers in good standing.

While this may sound punitive and extreme to modern ears, the main point is healing through confession and repentance before God, the abbot, and the brothers of the community. Then everyone at each level offers prayer and forgiveness. It is a vertical and horizontal action that cleans the slate to confession, repentance, and forgiveness. After that, the matter is settled, and the community can move forward without residual judgment or ill will. It doesn't just heal the offending brother, but all wronged by him, and the entire community as well.

Today a similar process is used in most monasteries. If a sin is private and not seen in the public forum, we encourage private monastic or sacramental confession between us and a spiritual director or priest. If a sin affects someone else, then we encourage a face-to-face meeting between the parties involved for humble confession and repentance, followed by loving forgiveness. If the conflict is so public that it involves the entire community, then we encourage public confession, repentance, and forgiveness before the entire community. We usually do this in a weekly public penance service, similar to what used to be called the chapter of faults. But instead of the emphasis being on faults, it is on reconciliation through repentance and mutual forgiveness so that one can move beyond them.

This may sound simple, but, believe me, it is far from easy! It is hard to humble oneself in confession. It is equally hard to humble oneself by praying for and forgiving one who may have offended or sinned against you personally.

Paul Simon once sang in a song, "I was wrong once, so I could be wrong again!" This is one of his typical Paul Simon witticisms, but it contains great truth. It's easy to point out the faults of others. It is most difficult to admit our own faults and sometimes even more difficult to forgive those of others. When we cannot forgive others, it is often hard to forgive ourselves. This sickness only compounds conflict after conflict and one bad relationship after another. It is like a snowball gathering up snow as it careens down a hill toward its own destruction.

Scripture says, "All have sinned and fallen short of the glory of God." News flash: This even includes us! Jesus says that we are not to look at other people's faults but first look to our own. Only then can we help others through the real motive of self-giving love. Otherwise, our so-called help might really be nothing more than an attempt to point out the faults of others and to aggrandize ourselves. This is an all-too-familiar religious disguise for self-will and ego in religious communities.

The Deeper Way Out

The way out of this negative relationship spiral is to let go of your old self, with all its ego-attached ideas and agendas, and die with Christ. Then the person God originally intended us to be will be born again through the resurrection of Christ. We will become a new creation, one that is free of ego attachments and has a healthy sense of the true self. We will have opinions and plans but not be attached to them. Then we can really listen to the opinions of others. Then we can freely share with others without arguing with or imposing our agendas and opinions on them. This is the way to healthy relationships.

Plus, when we have died to the old self, it is really easy to ask forgiveness for any wrongs or offenses we might have committed. If we are still hanging on to the ego-attached self, asking forgiveness is done with self-protective strings attached.

When we cut those strings through the cross of Christ, then we can ask and offer forgiveness freely. This heals most of the ills that plague relationships and resolves conflicts.

Dorotheus of Gaza describes a situation where another monk falsely accuses a brother. He says that the normal tendency is to defend oneself. But he says that in monasteries they learn that this is not the way to peace. We have learned the same thing. Most of us feel rather self-justified in almost anything we do, or we would not have done it. Monks are no exceptions. He says that the only way to peace is to take responsibility for one's own part in a broken relationship rather than accusing others. He calls it "self-accusation." What does this mean?

He says that even though you may not have directly done anything wrong to deserve the wrongdoing, there may be something in your relationship with the brother in the past that has festered within his heart and caused him to lash out and accuse you in the present. He goes even further and says that it may only be a subtly arrogant attitude or just a countenance on our part that causes the other monk to resent us, and so he strikes out against us. He says that we may not be as undeserving as we think and that we must take responsibility for our part in the broken relationship by confessing and asking forgiveness. This in turn may calm the other brother's anger and resentment and cause him to repent as well. The end result of mutual forgiveness is offered, and peace is reestablished. This usually resolves the conflict.

This process is far from easy. It demands great humility, not so much on the part of others, but on our part, even when we have been wronged. Our natural tendency is to self-justification in the name of justice. But that is not justice. The justice of Jesus is based on justifying others by giving up our own rights. It is about finding oneself by losing oneself for Jesus and his way of self-emptying love. Only then can we deal with other folks' problems without a self-agenda, regardless of how we try to tell ourselves and others that we are doing this for their own good or in the name of justice.

Communal Correction

This does not mean that we do not address real relational and other problems in community. The contrary is true. A loving monk and monastic community also correct the wrongs of others. If a parent does not correct a child, it leads the child to wrong habit patterns that cause real problems later on in life. A loving parent corrects. It is an unloving one that does not want to be bothered with the inconvenience of the energy and risk it takes to reach out. The same is true in a monastic community.

After practicing the self-accusation described above, Dorotheus actually says that it is most unloving not to help a brother monk through correction of sin. But it must be an act of selfless love. Not an act of self-justification. Once we let go of our self-will and pride, then we can address things for the sake of others rather than for ourselves.

It is like clearing the pond through sacred stillness. Only when the water of the pond is clear can we really see what is going on. Then we can really help. As Jesus says, "Remove the plank from your own eye before you try to remove the splinter from another's eye." At that point correction has nothing to do with self-justification.

But most ordinary folks are far from that reality. Even in monasteries, self-will and pride run free once a monk has learned to talk the monastic talk, stay under the radar of most trouble, and keep most of the rules. This is really very sad and keeps a monk from gathering the great riches of authentic monastic life. It causes one to exist in a monastery but not really live and thrive there. When this sickness goes untreated, it spreads throughout the monastery and creates a community of lukewarm monks who neither excel in monastic life nor allow others to do so either. It is a great and terrible tragedy.

Plus, it is my experience that the ones who really need to let go of their old self are often the ones who are convinced that they have got it right already. But they are often only the most religious and litigious. They are often still hanging on to themselves by being possessive of the very religion that is supposed to free them from it. They have learned to hide behind the very gift that God has given them to come out and step into the light in order to be fully healed in Christ. This is always tragic but is more common than one might think.

Probably the biggest mistake that people make in monasteries is trying to find inner peace by changing the people around them to fit their version of peace. We have addressed this above, but it takes on a most specific appearance in monasteries. Sometimes monastics love the outer trappings of monastic life and think that if they can get everyone else to adopt them the same way that they do, they can find monastic peace. That is an exercise in futility. No one, not even the ones we like and love the most, will ever be just like what we would like them to be. To try to do this is really trying to make them according to our image and likeness rather than God's. It is trying to be God.

The real key to the early monks was that they did not try to bring peace to the world by fixing the big bad world's problems. They had the humility to begin with themselves. Rather than seeing everyone else's sins, they focused on fixing their own. Then, they could help other monks with theirs.

And we must be patient. These changes do not happen overnight. We would love for the scriptural injunction to not let the sun go down on our wrath be true, for all our conflicts to be solved by nightfall. But usually it just doesn't work that way. Those who live in community for decades learn to be friends of time. Sometimes those you had the biggest problems with in the beginning become your friends after many years. They may not be your best spiritual friend or kindred spirit. But there will be a common understanding that years of mutual experience in monastic community bring that simply cannot be gotten any other way. I have learned to be a friend of time and have found peace.

Departure and Dismissal

But this does not mean that everyone should or does stay at the monastery. The Rule of St. Benedict allows for the dismissal of brothers who simply will not repent of recurring sin. This kind of behavior brings great agitation to the overall peace and tranquility of a monastic community. Sometimes, after repeated attempts to help the erring member, it is best that they leave. Usually they choose to do this on their own. On rare occasions the community must ask them to leave. In the Catholic Church there are definite laws that must be followed that ensure the rights of the individual and the community. It is never arbitrary or rushed. A real process of serious discernment is used.

The Rule of St. Benedict also allows the monastic community to accept those who wish to return. Sometimes it is apparent that a mistake was made by the departure. But this is not completely open-ended. After trying and failing several times, it does not allow readmission. In a sense they say that enough is enough. You either get it or you don't.

Most of those who follow the way of The Universal Monk in new forms of monasticism will not do so from actual monasteries. Most will associate with monasteries and meet in cell groups with others in the secular world at most. Many will only visit the monastery they associate with annually, monthly, or weekly. A few will go there more frequently. So the intensity of community life and the ensuing conflicts will be less frequent. But they will still arise on occasion. These principles still work well in these circumstances. Plus, the community of one's family provides ample opportunity to practice these universal principles of conflict resolution through the distinctly monastic way.

All of us face conflicts with others in life. The Universal Monk is no exception. Just embracing a monastic spirituality will not magically make them go "poof" and disappear. Real monastic spirituality is a way to bring Jesus to daily life. Give these ideas a try. You might find they work well for you. But you have to really let go of self. The cross and resurrection of Jesus provide a sure way to do that.

Leadership

Spiritual Fathers and Mothers and Elders

M onastic life and the mystical life of the Universal Monk is an integration of the inner and outer person that is very simple yet most complete. For the person going through it, it can sometimes feel most complex, even a bit confusing and overwhelming! That is why the monastic tradition strongly teaches that the average monk seeks some spiritual direction through a spiritual father or mother, as well as a rule of life and community. These leaders are usually called abbots and abbesses. They simply mean father and mother, respectively.

The Desert Fathers

The Desert Fathers and Mothers are representatives of some of the earliest Christian monasticism. They were seen as elders and fathers and mothers. An elder is an older sibling. A father or mother is one who actually helps conceive and train a spiritual child. The Desert Fathers and Mothers are older and wiser brothers and sisters who help the younger child along the way of Christ. But they also are part of "mother church" and help give birth to and further raise spiritual children in Christ.

These fathers and mothers usually did not try to set anything up too formally. They simply went into the desert to live as hermits and sooner or later attracted disciples when word got out that they were someone worth following. It all unfolded quite naturally. Even St. Pachomius, who set up large formal monasteries and leadership, only set himself up as leader after living as a hermit under a spiritual father and after trying a role of humbly doing the physical work for the others in the community he set up so that they could more exclusively pray and study. It was met by failure. His more formal leadership role as spiritual father was something that was both natural and necessary and confirmed by the local bishop.

Western Monasticism

Western monasticism came from that desert experience as a developed integration of the cenobitical monks of St. Pachomius's *koinonia* and the semi-eremitical hermits of St. Antony, the Father of Monks. There are many early rules, but the Rule of St. Benedict is the one that was eventually most widespread.

Toward the very beginning of the rule in chapter 2, Benedict treats the role of the abbot as something essential to monastic life. He treats it again toward the end of the rule in chapter 64, confirming and adding to what he already said at the beginning. Most scholars believe that it was probably added after years of experience.

The abbot (or abbess in the female tradition) is the spiritual father of the community. Some would say right off the bat that Jesus said to "call no man father." But St. Paul calls himself both a spiritual father and mother of the communities and individuals he helped birth in Christ. So it seems clear that the intent is not to put God's leaders before God himself. A real leader is to minister from their own life with God and help bring others back to God. They are only conduits. God the Father is the real spiritual water. Even Jesus always points the way to the Father in the Holy Spirit.

Interestingly, the early church also sometimes saw Jesus as the earthly spiritual father who leads all back to his Father in heaven. That was passed on to the early abbots. So, the abbot and abbess stand in the place of Christ to the monastic community. They do so as the "firstborn among many brothers" or as elder brothers and sisters and as spiritual parents.

While they stand in the place of Christ, they do not stand in the way of Christ. People must develop their own personal relationship with Christ. Indeed, the abbot and abbess are to guide them to that end alone. They are never to be the center of attention or the goal of a monk's obedient service.

The Model Abbot

The role of the abbot is foundational to the monastery. But he is not given a tyrannical scope. The Rule of St. Benedict's treatment of the ministry of the abbot is a great Leadership 101 for any leader of any group, religious or secular. They are not to be autocratic or dictatorial. They are supposed to apply their leadership in a way that meets the temperament and character of the person they are ministering to. With the humble they are to be soft and gentle. Most souls in monasteries fall into that category or they would not even want to be monks in the first place. Only with the rough and arrogant are they to be stern and strong. This is very similar to the Rule of Augustine where he states that all are treated equally but not identically when it comes to meeting the needs of all, for all have different needs. The good abbot moderates and adapts his leadership to each monk when ministering to him individually.

The abbot does not make all the decisions. He also listens to the council of seniors and the full assembly of monks in chapter. Even novices or new members can be used by the Spirit to speak to the community. There are also other roles of service such as the porter, cellarer (who looks after the physical stuff on the place), deans, the prior, and other elder monks who are even given the role of spiritual fatherhood at times. Yet, throughout the Rule of Benedict the role of the abbot and obedience to him are strongly emphasized. There is interplay between the will of the monks and the decision of the abbot.

Today, monasteries in the West use a rather standard combination of democracy and the decision of the abbot. The monks freely discuss monastery issues and take a vote on most things. There are also leadership councils and committees who report to the community and the abbot. Then the abbot decides. He has the final say, and the buck stops with him. But community constitutions clarify which things the abbot must have the support of the chapter for. These are usually not the ordinary things of daily monastic life but big issues like receiving new members into the community or starting new ministries and foundations. The other stuff is discussed in council and chapter and decided by the council and/or the abbot.

I remember a humorous story of how this sometimes plays out. An abbot sought the will of the community through a vote. When he heard the results, he solemnly said, "You have not heard the will of God. Vote again!" He couldn't rule without the vote. But the final decision was his. Within reason and the norms of monastic law, the specific tone is in the hands of the charism of each abbot. I am also reminded of my friend Abbot Jerome Kodell's book, simply titled *Don't Trust the Abbot*. It is filled with humorous wisdom about how an abbot and community must cooperate in order to have a working relationship that accomplishes the greater will of God.

Choice of the Abbot

The choice of the abbot is also interesting. By and large the founder in the first generation leads monasteries. They also act as spiritual fathers. But the history of how communities treat founders and foundresses is not always so kind. Often the community is ready for a new leader after the founder begins to age beyond usefulness. Regardless, upon the death of the spiritual father, abbot or abbess, a new one is chosen. This is usually done by the vote of the community itself. But chapter 64 of the Rule of Benedict addresses the case where a bad choice is made. It does not indicate whether the monks know that it actually was a bad choice. At that point the neighboring abbots and bishop may step in and help get a new one. In monastic history this sometimes meant bringing in a good leader from another monastery. A democratic choice is preferred, but it is not always accepted when it goes terribly wrong. It is not really specified how this all worked out practically.

Today there are some pretty specific protocols followed for the election of a new abbot. It involves not only the vote of a community but also its confirmation by the abbots of the congregation the monastery is a part of. The church confirms the election through the office of the bishop in which the monastery is located.

It is also good to note that there was a growing tendency to relegate the role of the abbot to a prelate and administrator of a rather large abbey. He became a spiritual father only in name and in general. The day in and day out spiritual direction was left to other monastery leaders who may or may not have had an official capacity. But all was done under the overall guidance and knowledge of the abbot and the seniors. And the abbot had the right to step into that relationship at any time if he felt it was going wrong.

St. Francis

Francis was the unquestioned spiritual father of the early Franciscan movement. In *Origins of the Franciscan Order*, the great Franciscan scholar Kajetan Esser said that Francis really carried on the monastic ideal of the spiritual father but broadened the scope of his authority to an entire international community. This was a radical shift. He did not want to be called "abbot" or even "prior" (the first among brothers) because of the pomp and pride that had come to be associated with these offices in his day. But he was the true spiritual father of the early friars.

The nature of that spiritual fatherhood changed. It was international and therefore more inspirational than a local pastor or spiritual director could be. He ministered to friars personally in the beginning and even to a select handful as the order grew. He was a minister general, or one who ministered to the general and overall concerns of the international community. Local and regional matters were left to the local guardians, or custos (custodians), and the provincial minister. The provincial became a kind of regional abbot or major superior, and the local leaders were more like monastery officials. But it had all taken on a larger perspective than just one local monastery.

Then he resigned his office as general minister. Some say that he did so because of poor health. The sources also hint that he did so out of frustration that the brothers no longer followed his counsel. Regardless, he no longer had any official capacity as the leader of the community. But he remained the founder and, all would say, the spiritual father.

The leadership of the Franciscans always had a strong democratic flavor to it. The friars met in chapters to learn and dialogue and to eventually vote on various issues. They especially had the right and obligation to vote for their leaders. The rule specifically mentions that the provincials are to elect the general minister. At first it was for life, as with the spiritual father tradition of traditional monasticism. They could be removed if they were found to be really bad leaders.

After some repeated and truly terrible experiences with bad general ministers, they eventually took to electing them for a term. Today, Franciscans vote for most major decisions and have a rather complex system of councils for leadership and election on provincial and international levels.

After the mendicant friars, the tendency in the West was toward a much more democratic leadership. Some communities, like the Carmelites, had already been founded by a group, rather than by one specific person. Only under later pressure from Rome did they list St. Bertold (the presumed first prior of the hermitage on Mount Carmel in the Holy Land) as their one founder. Seven original founders of the Servites are honored in the liturgical calendar today.

Eastern Christian Monasticism

The Eastern Christian monastic tradition is even stronger than the West concerning the spiritual father. This is seen especially with the practice of the Jesus Prayer, working through the eight vices with various spiritual and community practices, and finally coming into contemplation. In the East this is usually found in the head of a local community, or the hegumen. But the word really only means "the leader" or, some would say, to "point the way." Jesus said that he only pointed to the Father and that he was the way to him. (This is very similar to the Buddha, who said not to look at him because he was only a finger pointing to the moon, which is the real goal.) They are never the object or goal of the obedience of the disciple. There can also be other spiritual fathers or elders designated in the monastery. Some of them found sketes, or a small cottage or group of hermitages around a small house and chapel in greater seclusion but still dependent on a sponsoring monastery that is under a hegumen. You never set yourself up as a spiritual father. It simply happens when you are elected the hegumen or when monks start coming to you for spiritual direction. It is all quite natural and involves no arrogance or pride on the part of the spiritual father, though they can be quite exacting in their direction at times. The son obeys the father. Without the father the son is left to spiritually wander alone and often ends up lost and confused.

While we in the West have adopted many things from the Eastern tradition, we less frequently make use of the spiritual father or mother. Perhaps this is due to our more independent nature, even in monasteries. Or maybe it is because such holy people are harder to find in them! Either way, we are less concerned with this. But the Eastern monastics consider it absolutely essential. Basil Pennington reported that during his historic long-term visit to Mount Athos many there hesitated to publish the great Eastern monastic writings of the *Philokalia* in English due to this missing link in our approach to the spiritual life.

In the West we have tended to use the term "spiritual director." It is similar to the spiritual father or mother but not identical. Like the East, we go to them simply as ones who can help us along the spiritual path. They help us to avoid mistakes and to get out of trouble when we fall into a spiritual hole. It is never about them. It is about our relationship with God. They are only helpers.

But the East takes devotion and obedience to them more seriously. Though never treated as official leaders of the church, this role and relationship are simply taken for granted in good monasteries. Plus, just like an earthly father, a spiritual father is one for life. There is rarely a change from one to another. When they die, they remain your spiritual father, but the relationship changes and you live in obedience under the leaders of the monastery. If the monk is younger, he might find someone similar to help him on his way. If the monk is older, he usually becomes a spiritual father himself.

Eastern Religion

There is also something similar to this in the religions and monasteries of the Far East. In particular, Hinduism and Buddhism also have similar spiritual guides. The disciple is expected to find a guru to whom he offers complete obedience. But the relationship is entered into at the disciple's choosing and voluntarily. This is something quite mystical and precious. To find the right guru is a great gift, and, as they say, "When the disciple is ready, the master appears." In the end they are to "stand on the shoulders" of the guru and actually go up higher spiritually. This is similar to Jesus saying of us that "greater works will you do" when referring to the church. In Hinduism such teachers often attract disciples into ashrams or "communities." These contain both long-term and short-term members. In the more serious ashrams they are expected to live as celibates and without their property while they live there, even if they have husbands or wives.

In Zen Buddhism it is mandatory that one "find a good teacher." To try to get it from books or DVDs is simply impossible. Without the teacher, Zen meditation remains a dead parroting without transmitting the authentic spiritual life behind the often-demanding disciplines that really work. They also have communities where the teacher, or roshi, acts as leader. Buddhism in general is more essentially monastic than almost any other religion. But their monastic rule does not presume that the local leader will be a meditation teacher, though they often are. They are most democratic in the actual operation of the monastery.

Non-Catholic/Orthodox Christian

There are fewer non-Catholic or non-Orthodox Christian monastics than the above-mentioned traditions. There are even more non-Christian ones than what is found in Protestant and nondenominational Christianity. It tends to be a more lay and secular approach to the spiritual life lived in the secular world. But monks and monasteries are certainly not altogether absent either. There are some fine monasteries in Anglicanism, and even some are found among Lutherans. The New Monasticism is itself a term coined by a new community of Baptists using the Rule of St. Benedict as its foundational guide for community living. In most of these monasteries a rather traditional approach to monastic leadership is used. It pretty much mirrors that found in other more established Christian monasteries. This is true especially among the Anglicans.

But there are also some examples from the Anabaptist tradition of Plain People that are quasi-monastic and represent the inclusion of families in integrated monasteries. These tend to use a more democratic approach to leadership. This democracy can be for the entire congregation or for a group of elders in council. It can also be both. Many tend to rotate the role of leading Sunday worship, though some have a sort of ordained clergy nowadays. But the role of a central leader as spiritual father is much less evident in these approaches to community. Yet it is not absent either, especially in a community where the founder is still living. Among the Bruderhof, the role of Christoph Arnold, as the son of the founder, Eberhard Arnold, is still powerful. He is a holy man and is honored for his role in the community.

Of course the Protestant tradition runs the gamut on leadership models. It ranges from Congregationalists, where the congregation has the final say rather than the pastor, to more episcopal models where a district or local pastor is the final authority. These are called by different names and given different scopes of authority. The monastic expressions of these communions understandably take on the character of their base communion. But sometimes completely interfaith groups like Taizé are free to use their own structure based on a more broad tradition.

Today

I tend to delegate a lot of pastoral authority today. When we started, I had to do just about everything, from general administration to pastoral ministry receiving and forming new members to my ongoing music and teaching ministry that supported the community. Much like the young Pachomius, I was financially supporting the community. I simply could not sustain it, and the community needed to learn to support and guide itself. Today each group and work section in the monastery is run by respective leaders that are appointed on the consideration of the will of the community through individual consultation. The head of each respective group, celibate men, women, singles, and families, does formation of new members. I am available for counsel when the delegated leaders cannot minister to a situation or person. This delegation has greatly helped to streamline the leadership of the community.

There are two main models of community leadership today. There is the traditional monastic model of primary and delegated leaders who meet in council and the general membership who meet in gatherings or chapters. This is a rather traditional and tested model of leadership. The role of spiritual father or mother is maintained with this model and adapted to modern circumstances.

There is also a rather group-styled leadership where most everything is decided by the group. The leader is really more of a group facilitator than a primary spiritual leader. This approach makes everyone feel very involved but requires a lot of time in group meetings for processing. Many new communities are smaller so simply do not have the time. On the other hand, where making a living is not so important and the community lives through donations, a smaller community is better equipped for the kind of meetings this approach requires.

Our Community

In the history of Little Portion Hermitage we have tried both. We have settled on the more monastic approach. In the beginning we had a weekly meeting where we voted on almost everything. I remember that we even voted on what kind of dog food to buy! It required a lot of time for dialogue. We used the classical meeting primer, *Robert's Rules of Order*. As founder I was just one of the gang, though I was the founder and only real breadwinner. Our budget skyrocketed, and discipline in community was pretty lax. Many outside observers saw that I was being taken advantage of by well-meaning folks. We had gotten stuck in a quasi-monasticism that simply didn't work.

So we switched to the more monastic model. As the one who attracted most vocations and who had written the original rule of life, I was recognized as the founder and clear leader of the group. We attracted large numbers of vocations and developed delegated leaders, a council, work heads, and community meetings. In the early days I was still pretty involved on most every level. As time went on, I delegated more authority so that I could better devote my time to general leadership, greater solitude, and outside ministry. It is not perfect, but it tends to get the job done.

We still hear that some folks don't feel they get to participate enough or that there is not enough dialogue. We also hear that some think there is too much time in meetings and want more time for either work or prayer. We hear it all. We continually try to work on this when we hear it. Often those who want more meetings for input are folks who have a hard time relinquishing control of their lives under the leadership of another. Sometimes the ones who complain the most are actually the ones that the other community members think are the most dictatorial when in any kind of position of authority. They are sometimes the most feared by other community members, though they tend not to frighten me. This continues to be a topic we give a lot of attention to when it comes up. But it comes up less and less as we grow as a community.

Probably the hardest thing for a new community is the smallness of numbers and the amount of work to be done. Most strong members wear several hats. Only the weaker ones or the new ones wear only one. Consequently, most members are very busy. Trying to get all the work done and spend time on formation and prayer is a real challenge on many days. Perhaps that is why we opted for the more monastic model of leadership. The thought of longer community meetings and lots more energy expended for processing more things is really repugnant to most of our folks.

My Personal Experience

In my personal ministry as founder and spiritual father, I find that I spend most of my time in conference simply listening to others. As I listen, I pray. I try to meditate so that I can hear not only what they are saying but also their spirit. Then I respond. I try not to react, even when I hear some truly outrageous things! Reacting rarely gets anything accomplished. So I share softly with most folks, even when I have to correct them. Some are simply not ready to be corrected at all. So, I wait for a better time. Some will never be able to be corrected or receive it with a humble spirit. They have not learned to listen. These do not make it in community. And some are older and past the point in their lives where any serious behavioral change will occur. They have already made many sacrifices in other areas in community and have done their bit. We simply learn to love them as they are.

But I am not afraid to speak strongly when someone is beating around the bush, or trying to defend him or herself. I am most clear that what I teach is a complete renunciation of the old self and a resurrection of a new person in Christ. All

I teach is the cross of Christ, nothing less and nothing more. It is an uncompromised message of living out the cross and resurrection of Jesus in a monastic community setting. It is simple but most challenging. Usually the message itself is strong enough on its own without me having to emphasize it too much!

I also try to get to the point and stay with it. I have found that long sessions usually get nowhere. They also just wear both the individual and me out. By the end of too much talk I am simply too weary to give any good input. So I encourage folks to have their thoughts as organized as possible when they see me. I also ask them not to try to cover everything in one session. Usually thirty minutes is a good amount of time to spend on a regular basis. Occasionally I will go one hour. Anything more than that becomes counterproductive.

Finally, it has taken me years to get to the point where I am really comfortable with this role of leadership. In the beginning I was often awkward. I was too soft or too hard. I said too much or too little. I am not a born leader, so I learned things the hard way. I made a lot of mistakes. Had I only been allowed one or two six-year terms in office, I probably would not have had the time to get the hang of it. A life term works well for me and probably for most founders. But I must admit that now that I am beginning to get to know the job, I am also getting a bit old for it! These long years of learning by trial and error have taken their toll. I am ready to just retire to a hermitage and go out from there to fulfill an even more general role with the entire community, monastic and domestic, and spread the gospel in the parishes. I am sure that the next generation will do a much better job than I have!

This is a topic that will be most relevant for most new communities of the New Monasticism who live in actual monasteries. This applies to integrated and to more traditional models. These principles also apply to those who live in their own homes but associate with monasteries as domestics, oblates, seculars, or associates. While the obedience is not as specific in their case, it is no less real when it comes to the spiritual life.

Ministry

We have a very ministry-minded approach to life in the church today. Pope Paul VI went so far as to say that the church actually exits to evangelize, and John Paul II initiated what he called "the new evangelization." They are right. Many folks immediately ask about our new monastic community, "What is your ministry?" But the monastic and Franciscan traditions do not specify a particular ministry. They simply assume that one uses whatever gifts they have for the greater glory of God and that is a ministry in itself. A deeper reading of the above-mentioned papal references to ministry also reveals the same attitude.

The first monks would never have considered the question of ministry. They simply lived the gospel. That was ministry enough. They generally did not engage in preaching because they witnessed so much arrogance and pride on the part of the preachers and clerics in the diocesan and parish churches. In fact, they said that monks should flee ordination as one would flee a woman trying to tempt them away from the monastic life. Only a few were ordained to minister the sacraments to the other monks.

But they did teach and preach to other monks and seekers of the monastic way. The earliest monastic sources reveal that quite a bit of time was devoted to spiritual conferences.

Some were private, and some were as a group. *The Sayings of the Desert Fathers* is a classic, as are the *Institutes* and *Conferences* of John Cassian.

They also had contact with the outside world. Regardless of all their language of "fleeing the world," they still lived in it. They had to make a living just like everyone else. Mostly they made baskets and plaited ropes during their prayer time and sold them to the people in the towns around them. Sometimes they destroyed them once they had served their purpose as a meditation tool to keep the hands busy while occupying their minds and hearts in prayer. But they also made a living by producing and selling them to non-monastics as a sort of cottage industry.

There is also evidence of more serious industry. We know that the monks had to travel on boats for business and even had their own barge to take their crafts downstream to Alexandria and other towns along the Nile. In the more communal cenobitical monasticism, St. Pachomius housed the monks in groups of ten based on their craft and trade. He had houses for bakers, potters, farmers, and so on. The monastery was large, some say as many as thousands of monks, though some modern scholars doubt that number. Nonetheless, they were veritable cities in the desert. Forms of industry and self-support were absolutely necessary. This involved interaction with outsiders, and this implied ministry. The first monks were encouraged to sell their goods at a somewhat lower price than the worldly traders in order to minister to those who could not normally afford various items. This was also pretty smart marketing!

There were also some preachers. While this was generally left to the secular clergy, we see St. Antony himself going to Alexandria to preach when the Marconian and Arian heresies were threatening the church. Bishop Athanasius was a friend, so he felt obligated to go and help him in his struggle to preserve the correct teaching about Jesus. Antony encouraged those suffering martyrdom as well, going so far as to become a threat to court proceedings. That was "social action" in its own day. By the way, most scholars believe that the Arians were archconservatives, believing only a more literal and conservative reading of Scripture. Athanasius was more progressive, preaching a healthy development of the teaching of Scripture in the hypostatic union of full divinity and humanity, as well as the various operations and characters (economies) of the persons of the Trinity. Antony was best known as a holy hermit and monastic founder. That was a ministry in itself. But he also ventured into the world to preach and do social justice when there was a genuine need, and he was truly called by the Spirit to respond.

In Western monasticism the Rule of Benedict applies early monasticism to its contemporary Southern European environment. It also allows those with various trades to practice them, as long as they do not get puffed up with pride because of their work. He also mentions selling crafts at a somewhat lower price. But he wants the enclosure of the monastery maintained so that monks do not go out unnecessarily. He wants everything necessary for the monastery's support to be produced from inside. Some trips outside were necessary, and he allows for it in his encouragement of better habits for those traveling outside. But he wants the monks to return them once they return. It is never considered that they would be gone too long, perhaps no more than a day-trip. He generally does not allow traveling monks to eat outside of the enclosure. Perhaps because of this, the later monks became rather famous, or some would say infamous, for allowing great fairs on abbey grounds, where craftsmen and traders would come from all around. Monks would also participate, and the monastery got a fair payment for this service as well!

A similar development took place in the Christian monastic East. But Neilos the Ascetic rather roundly condemns the monks for getting too involved in agriculture. He recommends that they get rid of their flocks and herds and return to the more rugged monastic life of the ancient desert that was extremely poor and therefore had little overhead and little need for much work other than prayer. It is an ongoing tension that shows up in all monastic circles every couple of hundred years.

But there were also great monastic preachers. Most were also voluminous writers. Many of the church fathers like Basil or Augustine were also monastics. John Chrysostom began as a hermit. Later, Augustine of Canterbury was the great missionary to Britain. Boniface was the great missionary to Germany. Then, of course, there was St. Bernard of Clairvaux. He was undoubtedly the most well-known and powerful churchman of his time. Yet, he was also the abbot of an abbey of the Cistercian reform of the Benedictines. Some say that he spent as much as 80 percent of his time away preaching and teaching. St. Romuald was not a popular preacher, but he founded many monasteries and reformed still more during his life of one hundred plus years. He was a hermit who traveled and called everyone to monastic life simply by living it. St. Peter Damien was part of the Romualdian, or Camaldolese, movement and was also one of the most popular preachers of his time. It is said that he wanted to make the entire world a monastery! Many popes were monastics first. Perhaps the greatest of these is St. Gregory the Great. These are all great monastic preachers and ministers.

Monasteries were also known as places where the poor would be given care through various ministries. Pilgrims' hostels were common in many monasteries. Every monastery was encouraged to give plenty of food and clothing to the poor of its local area. The monastery cared for the sick and provided jobs. The monastic industries employed many people from outside of the monastery to help with monastery industry and building. They also provided education for children, though this was primarily for the higher class, whose sons and daughters were expected to be better educated for their eventual role in society. Some stayed on and became clerics. The poor families could allow their children to be trained in an abbey to become a monk when they came of age. It was a pretty good option in an otherwise bleak social environment for the poorer folks. These were all "social programs" in their own day. They provide powerful examples for monastic ministry today!

In the Benedictine tradition the Camaldolese employ what they call the "threefold good." This means that, based on the pattern of St. Romuald, a monk can transition from the cenobium to the hermitage to ministry. That ministry can involve itinerant traveling in a style much like the pilgrims of the West or the sannyasi of the Far East. It may or may not include preaching. But hermit preachers began to be raised up by the Spirit. Many simply became part of the more informal and ancient penitential movement that was regaining popularity at the time. Some joined or founded new semi-eremitical communities. They all paved the way for the mendicants.

The mendicants of the thirteenth century seriously expanded the scope and mode of these ministries. Making the world their cloister, their bodies their cell, and their souls the hermit within, the friars became traveling monasteries of sorts, taking the gospel to everyone wherever they might be. St. Francis and St. Dominic became the two great models of this movement, though there were many more. There were many preachers, to be sure, but their ministry was simply to use whatever gift each one had in order to bring the love of Jesus to others. While Dominic's Order of Friars Preachers was more specifically geared to preaching, the Franciscans used a more grassroots definition of ministry. They worked alongside common laborers, ran leprosariums, and even begged alongside the poor when they could not find work. Francis is now known as an *alter Christus*, or "another Christ," and a most apostolic man. But he was also known for doing manual labor, rebuilding and sweeping out churches, and begging with the beggars that were so common in those days.

He is also known as the patron saint of ecology. Francis' beautiful *Canticle of the Creatures* and his teaching to make of all creation a ladder by which to ascend to the presence of God are primary. He called God the divine Artist that can be seen in all the works of art in creation if one has the eyes of faith to see. This inspired St. Bonaventure's *Itinerarium*, or *Journey of the Soul to God*. Within it he said that all creation bears God's traces and all humanity bears God's image. Therefore, we must have a great love and respect for all creation as God's traces, or we dishonor God. We especially love and respect human life, which bears God's own image, or we dishonor God's divine image in humanity. That will change the way we treat one another!

When the Franciscans began to settle down in established "places," they almost invariably founded little hermitages based on the semi-eremitical pattern of the desert. This consisted of a church and a common house, with hermit cells scattered around far enough away to provide solitude but close enough to gather for meals and some common prayer. They had a small impact on the local ecology until and even after the fourteenth- to fifteenth-century Observant Reform of St. Bernadine, who built most of the quaint Franciscan structures we see in Italy today. They usually had a small vegetable and herb garden but got most of their supplies from the alms of folks in a nearby town. The environmental impact was small. And many ministries went forth from them to nearby towns.

The Benedictine pattern is more significant. Benedict wanted everything needed for the monk's life to be produced from the monastery itself. There was a complete ecology produced from a big monastery. Farming, arts and crafts, education, illuminating manuscripts, and much more were carried on within a large monastery of the middle ages. When run correctly, the monastery had a positive effect on the people and the ecology of the local area. This had special significance during the Dark Ages, when the political and environmental health of Europe was in trouble. Monasticism is sometimes credited with keeping civilization alive as it preserved and passed on the wisdom of the past and helped shape a better future. Monastics helped many of the agricultural developments that literally restored Europe after the Dark Ages. Things like the modern plow were developed by the monasteries to help feed a starving population.

When done wrongly, it could destroy the ecology of an entire region, and that sometimes happened. The spread of Cistercian monasteries and the sheep industry they developed did real economic and environmental harm in Britain and Ireland. But most of the time it was a force for great good.

Today monasteries are getting seriously involved in environmental issues. They are using their lands for organic farming and gardening and putting in alternate energy sources such as wind generators and passive and active solar collectors. Franciscans are doing the same, though it is more difficult with a local community that is in and out a lot with various outside ministries. But even the Franciscans used to operate farms in conjunction with their larger houses in America, though many of these have now been sold due to the lack of friars to populate them.

We started an ecological and agricultural aspect to our community from the beginning at Little Portion Hermitage. We grow almost all our own food in natural sustainable agriculture and have beautiful prayer gardens. We also operate a free-range poultry business. We do not yet produce our own energy, though we do use energy-saving practices throughout the monastery buildings and grounds. We also try to buy and sell locally whenever possible. This all seems most Benedictine, with its monastic stability and self-sufficiency.

Most Benedictine monasteries today are engaged in more traditional outside ministries as well. Some do parish work, much like the mendicant orders, by becoming pastors and ministers. Many American monasteries are also involved in education. They operate monastic schools ranging from boarding schools to universities. But the primacy of contemplation is conscientiously strived for by all.

We also do some significant outside ministry from Little Portion. Of course, I do my JMT ministries in published music, books, and an itinerant ministry of spiritual music, motivational speaking, and guided Christian meditation. But we also operate a successful retreat ministry at Little Portion Retreat Center over the hill from the Hermitage. In our history we also helped found the local Loaves and Fishes Food Bank and the Little Flower Clinic for those in our local area without health insurance. Since we had many members with teaching backgrounds, we tried to get an individualized (or adapted Montessori) Catholic school started, but it proved to be a bit ahead of its time in this area. We also have been most instrumental in the founding years of Mercy Corps, an international relief and development agency based in Portland, Oregon. This has all kept a small new monastic community pretty busy!

We have definitely felt the tension between local stabilized ministries, especially the ones requiring alternative agriculture and so on, and those that take us outside of the monastery. The heart of the tension is that local stabilized ministries need people at home on a daily basis to run them. The outside ministries take folks away from the monastery for significant periods of time. This is most true of itinerant ministry teams that go from parish to parish around the country or even around the world. If you do not have a large community, it is difficult to maintain both.

This is a typical tension based on the difference between monastic and mendicant, or Benedictine and Franciscan, styles of ministry. Most of the new monastic communities find that they do a little of both. If anything, they tend more toward direct evangelical ministries instead of the more traditional monastic model. The alternative environmental model is almost an add-on to more traditional ministries.

We have used an analogy of symptoms and causes to keep some of this straight. It is like a person who is sick. When one goes to the doctor's office, the first thing done is to relieve the pain. You anesthetize it. Then you can get to work on setting bones or doing surgery. If you try to do that first, the patient is too agitated to stay still, or the pain itself might kill them. You must first kill the immediate pain; then you do the surgery. You get to the cause of the problem. One relieves the immediate pain. The other gets to the long-term problem. We need both.

Many ministries deal with immediate pain. You evangelize but do not go into deep prayer and meditation. You lead with initial conversion but do not take them into ongoing conversion. You feed the poor but do not yet teach them how to farm. All these rather normal active ministries deal with the immediate pain. But they do not always get to the deeper problems. As they say in relief and development, give a person a fish, and you feed them for day. Give them a fishing pole and teach them how to fish, and you feed them for life.

The monastic model can solve many of these problems. These issues run deep and challenge much of the basic fabric of usually accepted patterns of modern living. The monastic model has the opportunity to be an alternative model of society alongside and within modern society.

Most of this has to do with a rural or urban-based lifestyle. The rural provides most of the essential basics of human needs. What are they? We all need food, clothing, shelter, energy, and entertainment, plus the religious and secular education to do these things. The urban is based more on providing for specialization and wants. The city is the place for specialization. It is meant to augment the mainstream of society that provides everyone's basic needs. When we become urban-based and provide mainly wants, then we become very close to forgetting how to produce our basic needs. This places the entire civilization in jeopardy.

It also has vast environmental ramifications. Back in the early 1970s, organic gardening sources said that before World War I, twenty-four out of every twenty-five families in America lived on a farm. After World War II, it had reversed. *Time* magazine once said that by 1983 it had escalated to forty-nine out of every fifty families now live in the city. This means that the minority of the population is producing the basic food that the majority needs. Where once farms were about 150 acres and farmed by a large family, now they are 3,000 acres and are farmed by a small family. This means farmers must use agribusiness methods of farming that are environmentally harmful. It also means that we must ship our food thousands of miles to give the average family a balanced diet, so we must use preservatives and coloring to make it look fresh. The result? It is unhealthy to grow it and unhealthy to eat it.

The environmental model of monasticism goes to the heart of the problems of Western civilization. It ranges from a relationship to God to relationships with each other to relationships with creation. It addresses how we make a living, how we affect each other globally, and how we affect the entire planet. It provides a basic stable base from which can flow various kinds of ministries. These include traditional ministries and new ones as well. In my heart of hearts I believe that this old monastic pattern may have the greatest thing to offer an increasingly artificial culture. I am personally involved in bringing that message to others through teaching and preaching. But it is the example of the integrated monastery that makes those words a reality.

For those who do not live in new or old monasteries, there are still powerful ways to share in this monastic ministry. You can live as a domestic, oblate, or associate of a monastery. The very act of associating with monasteries while still living in the world gives you an exciting chance to share that monastic charism with the world. You will enter into prayer and be able to lead others in it. Start a meditation group. Pray the Liturgy of the Hours with others in your parish. Get involved with any active ministry in the parish or diocese but with a deeper monastic base that gives you contemplative peace and spiritual power. Mostly, love your family and treat them as your primary spiritual community. They are the domestic church and the most basic unit of civilization. On the ecological level, start a garden and grow some of your own food. You'll be surprised how much better it tastes and how much better it will be for you. Cut down on energy consumption and try to produce some of your own energy through things like solar panels or a wind generator. The government is actually giving tax breaks to those who do these things. These are just a few of a multitude of great possibilities out there for anyone who really wants to minister the love of God.

But there is one last way of ministry that is common to all and deeper than any external form of ministry. It is the way of real contemplative prayer. This is the final solution for everyone, for those who live in monasteries and those who don't. It is the way of the Universal Monk. Once you do this, you begin to see that the entire world is a monastery. Like Francis, the world becomes our cloister, our bodies our cell, and our soul the hermit within. We become a living meditation.

On this level, we solve every problem created by sin by being healed of it and moving beyond it. Here we simply become one with the One who created everything. We learn to be with the One who *is*. We regain something of that original unity that existed in the primordial garden before the separation of ourselves from God, each other, and all creation by sin. By this simple act of oneness we pray every prayer that can be prayed and give spiritual power to every ministry that can be done. The way of the Universal Monk and the New Monastics is really the final answer for everyone. But it has existed from the beginning and is in every genuinely monastic community and all those united with them through desire or association. It is the way that renounces all to gain everything. It is the way that is separated from and united with all. This is the greatest ministry of all.

Appendix 1
Socioreligious Perspectives

Over the last seven or eight years my wife Viola and I have had the great opportunity to participate in several meetings about new forms of monastic and consecrated life that have been most helpful. These meetings were opportunities for dialogue, challenge, and cross-pollinating the best found in various groups. I would like to share a few points that might be helpful to our discussion.

A few years ago Viola and I met Sr. Patricia Wittberg, SC, who gave an excellent sociological presentation on new forms of communities of consecration and consecration of life for the Congress of New Consecrated Communities in Rome. In her excellent book *Pathways to Recreating Religious Communities*, Sr. Patricia makes many points that are most relevant to the Universal Monk and the way of the New Monastics. She treats the phenomenon of new forms of community in the consecrated or religious/monastic tradition. Some of these are new, some are new within existing families such as Benedictine or Franciscan, and some are from within the actual structure of preexisting older communities. All are included in the Universal Monasticism.

We also participated in a presentation on integrated Monasticism for the general chapter of the American-Cassinese

Congregation of Benedictine monasteries. In our consultation to prepare for the chapter, we were asked to read about five or so books on the utopian movements of the nineteenth century in America. It was a fascinating study on what worked and what didn't. Beyond some of the apparent aberrations of these groups, there were several points that made good sense to me and that seriously affected the initial rise and the fall of most of these communities.

Finally, we participated as nonpresenters in the Monastic Institute at Saint John's University in Collegeville, Minnesota, a few years ago that treated the topic of new communities. It was also a great time of cross-pollinating with others. In fact, it was there that I met one of the founders of the New Monasticism among the Baptist tradition. Such opportunities are valuable beyond dollars invested or what mere words can describe.

Out of the many things discussed, I would like to mention a few of the points from which we learned. These include the different ways to join a new community, the need for clear boundaries between the community and the secular world and between various expressions of the community itself, and genuine enthusiasm for the continuation of the life.

All States of Life

It is clear that there is a new movement underway that includes those from all states of life. While some communities follow a more traditional model of celibate men and/or women only, most involve families as well. Some of these stay in their own homes while others live in intentional community in a quasi-monastic geographical setting on one monastic campus or compound.

This is both ancient and new. In ancient days, families often joined monasteries but had to live as celibates to do so. The children were raised by monastics in the school. The Celts allowed families on the monastic compound. Most monasteries allowed for families as workers who sometimes actually affiliated with the monastery in some way. "Oblates" first included only children donated, or "oblated," to the monastery by families but included adults after the time of the third orders of most mendicants in the thirteenth century.

In addition to having ancient roots, this is a relatively new phenomenon today. This development requires clarity as to how one joins and what the rights and responsibilities of each member include. Old models generally do not work. For instance, the third orders, oblates, and even new associates are not full members of the monastic community. They can sometimes feel that they are merely "add-ons." They do much of the work as employees or volunteers but are not required for community functions and do not have a voice in community decisions. But most of these folks would gladly join in a more meaningful capacity if they had the opportunity to do so.

In our community we have very clear legislation about how each member joins and how each participates. Within the monastery we have celibate brotherhood, sisterhood, singles who can marry, and families. We also have domestics who live in their own homes. But all are full members of the community. Each is given responsibilities that are appropriate for his or her state of life in or outside the monastery. We all profess the evangelical counsels (poverty, chastity, and obedience) but in ways appropriate to our states of life. And each expression is represented in both the general chapter that meets every five years and decides the major direction of the community and the general council that meets weekly and applies those directions in an ongoing way. This is revolutionary in the development of monastic life.

This also affects our use of terms. Since "consecrated life" properly refers only to celibates, we speak of "consecration *of* life." The same is true of the words monk or nun. Since these words generally refer to celibates only, we tend not to use these words to describe the single, married monastic, or domestic members. We refer to those in the integrated monastery as "monastics." We call only celibates "monks." We tend to call our consecrated sisters "sisters." Likewise, the titles "abbot" and "abbess" are historically reserved for celibate men or women who lead monastic communities. Since Viola and I are a married couple we are simply referred to as the spiritual father and mother. This is more understandable in today's world. Though even this requires explanation.

Boundaries

Many have argued for more porous boundaries between community and the secular world. This is a legitimate part of being cultural, or "in culture." But communities are also called to be "countercultural." We need to maintain a balance between the two. This requires clear boundaries. In our study of nineteenth-century utopian communities in America, it was apparent from the source material that the more clear the boundaries were, the more successful the communities were, and the less clear, the more the communities simply dissolved. The more like the secular world they became, the less successful they were. The more countercultural they were, the more people joined and stayed.

In the general directory of the BSC, we address the issue of cultural and countercultural regarding our approach to study, saying:

> In the study of secular or religious arts and sciences, the brothers and sisters are always faithful to the Christian worldview, which is incarnational, but can also be countercultural. Even when a predominant worldview is in conflict with the teaching of the gospel and the church, the brothers and sisters are called upon and are not ashamed to take a stand that is obedient to the church, becoming countercultural and nonconformists to the world.

We also explain the clear rights and responsibilities of each member within each particular expression of the community. It sounds rather complicated at first, but it is all pretty simple when viewed with some common sense. It is also most helpful and downright necessary in order to keep the community from disintegrating into a vague communal soup that is everything and nothing.

In today's experience of consecrated life, the same is true. Many monks and consecrated persons have adopted a more secular lifestyle as serious Christians in an attempt to be present to the secular world. This is certainly not wrong, but it can be confusing for members and prospective members alike. Those who wear secular dress, live in apartments, hold down professional jobs, and meet in community only weekly or monthly are certainly doing something commendable. But it can be a challenge to maintain a community with a clear vision. Often members of those communities are hard-pressed to identify that which distinguishes them from the secular faithful or from their associate members.

I have often heard it said that if young people want to join a monastic community, they want it to be clearly countercultural enough to warrant the sacrifice. Otherwise, why not live a similar life in the world and get to raise a family as well? Granted, such observations from those who have not yet lived in community can seem a bit naïve to those of us who have done so for decades, but we have to admit that there is some truth to their observations.

The new forms of intentional monastic life tend to be clearer in their lifestyle expressions. They live in community, wear a monastic habit of some sort, pray and mediate daily in private and in common, and abstain from many non-monastic secular involvements. These communities are growing. The ones that have opted for a more secular model are not. There is a real danger of some of these more clearly monastic or consecrated communities lapsing into fundamentalism or externalism in their countercultural stance, but most do so with a relatively informed sense of balance and equilibrium. Those who live in their own homes do so as well, but in an appropriately adopted fashion. Those who have no association with a monastic community and still attempt such monastic affections often suffer from a sense of deprivation and can even lapse into individualistic delusion without a tangible check and balance through contact with a like-minded and more experienced monastic.

Enthusiasm and Recruitment

Clear boundaries also make for clear enthusiasm about a life that is clearly understood. Lack of clarity brings lethargy and disappointment. Communities that have something to hold on to are more enthusiastic. That enthusiasm is infectious. It attracts folks who are seeking the same thing. And they are out there! We have only to look. We have only to raise the banner and say, "Come and join us!" You will be surprised how many will.

"Enthusiasm" has a root meaning of *en Theos*, or "in God." God says, "A nation of firm purpose you keep in peace." And, "You will know the truth, and the truth will set you free." For Christians, Jesus is "the way, the truth, and the life." While the deeper stuff of contemplative prayer and mysticism are paradoxical and beyond description, the beginnings must be clear or no one will be able to find the way. Clarity and enthusiasm call people to any unique lifestyle or ministry. Monasticism is no exception.

In itinerant ministry I have found that folks often just need someone to raise the banner and cry out, "This way, follow me," in order to follow. They want to respond, but often there is no one sending out the call. I am just foolish enough to actually do it! Even in today's environment that is less than friendly to religious vocations, many respond.

At the same time, no matter how much enthusiasm an evangelist or vocation director has, if the community does not also posses it, those who come to investigate our way of life will simply be repulsed. I have seen this in even the best communities. It has happened in ours. I am in itinerant ministry most of the year. Like St. Peter Damien of the eleventh century, I have been accused of wanting to make the entire world a monastery! No doubt, I love the life and believe in it thoroughly. But no matter how many I attract, if my home community does not have enthusiasm and joy, then all my work is in vain.

Sr. Patricia Wittberg encourages something radical here. She encourages each member to "tithe" ten hours a week to recruitment. With the work schedule at the hermitage, this sounds almost immediately undoable. But it can take many forms that make our current duties forms of evangelization if they are done with an evangelistic spirit. It can be active preaching or just spending time with young people. But she says that it must be done. Without it, most new communities will simply lose members and eventually die. But this takes genuine enthusiasm on the part of the members of the new communities themselves. It is not enough for the founders or leaders to be the only ones doing it. If the product is not good, no amount of good PR will keep a community alive.

In today's environment we simply cannot take vocations for granted. In days not so long ago families, Catholic schools, bishops, and local pastors did foster them. Not anymore. The murky waters of malaise and cloudy non-clarity, plus the recent sexual abuse scandals in the clergy and consecrated life, have greatly hindered the call. But it is still there! And faithful clergy and monastics are still there as well! The New Monasticism is about living the gospel clearly for all states of life and sending out that clarion call again.

Some would object that we are not about numbers. On one level this is true. On another level it is not. On one level we should mainly be concerned with just living the life and letting that be enough to call folks to follow. Plus, there is a radical monastic tradition that actually shuns vocational work in an effort to allow only those really called to even investigate, much less enter, the monastic life. The Carthusians make it downright difficult to join, and they still get the few they really want as members. No doubt, the Desert Fathers and Mothers did not recruit, yet their numbers grew at a phenomenal rate. This was a sovereign work of God. Human efforts of vocational recruitment can get in the way of the deeper work of the Spirit.

On another level it is dangerous and deadly to think this way. If you have good news, you must share it. Jesus actually commands us to do so! Plus, in order to have any real effect on the church or the world, we must have at least enough members to make a mark. The mark need not be huge in order to be leaven in the dough, but it must be significant enough to start the process. To ignore this dynamic dooms a community to a slow and painful death.

Relationship with the Church and Canonical Development

Some new communities take their relationship with the church for granted. While this can be seen as a genuine attitude of detachment from individual or communal ego, it can also be deadly. Pretty early on in our community's development we sought input from older friars and monks who helped us to take steps to establish a formal avenue of dialogue with the church and other communities of the church. We owe them a great debt of gratitude for their advice and assistance. This dialogue took two traditional forms.

The first was a good working relationship with our bishop and a legal, canonical establishment in the church. The second was to ask for a monastic visitator to give input to the community on a regular basis. We also sought out relationships with other old and new communities through visits and attending gatherings and conferences. Without these points of contact and dialogue, our community would remain at the outer periphery of the church and would be far less effective than we are with them.

The canonical development is of special interest. Currently there is no great place in canon law for integrated monasteries like ours. There is a good category for communities of consecrated life (what used to be called religious life), societies of apostolic life, secular institutes, and individual consecrated virgins and hermits. There is also one for laypeople as associations of the faithful. But there really is not a good place for a fully integrated community that includes both consecrated monastics and laypeople in one community. Current legislation either separates them into different communities or does not grant the consecrated persons the public recognition they really deserve.

In light of these limited choices, our community exists as an association of the faithful. Many similar communities do the same. There are two further choices here. You can either be a "private" or "public" association. A private association is recognized by the church but does not represent her in its lifestyle, worship, and ministry. A public association is both recognized by the church and represents her in its lifestyle, worship, and ministries. The only rub is that private associations may include non-Catholics and public associations cannot. This is because it is unfair to ask a non-Catholic to represent a church he or she does not buy into or belong to. We currently get around this by distinguishing the canonical Catholic community and non-Catholic participants. Non-Catholics participate in every way that does not require Catholic belief and practice. It protects the integrity of everyone while still allowing for genuine ecumenical involvement. It has worked out well for us on the pastoral level.

We believe there needs to be a new category in the next draft of canon law to more rightly accommodate integrated monastic and consecrated communities. It falls between traditional consecrated life and associations of the faithful. We call this consecration *of* life to distinguish it from traditional consecrated life. Both ask all members to profess the evangelical counsels but in a way proper to their state of life.

There is certainly no reason that the church could not do this. In the recent 1983 Code of Canon Law, it provided a place for societies of apostolic life and secular institutes for the first time, even though they had existed for a couple of hundred years. Until then they has all existed in a kind of canonical no man's land. They even resurrected the ancient categories of consecrated virgins and hermits, or anchorites and anchoresses. We believe that the next draft should include a new category for integrated communities of consecration of life or some title to that effect. The time has come for this new and exciting development.

A formal visitor or visitator is a great idea for a new community. But you must find the right one or it can be hurtful. A visitor literally visits the community once every year to do a check of how it is doing. Ours does confidential meetings with leadership and each member. The leadership provides a general financial report (the diocese gets a written one annually) and an overview of the community's spiritual, emotional, and physical health. The visitor gives a report to the community and another one to the bishop at the conclusion of the visitation. These include confirmations, corrections, and challenges. They are really most encouraging.

We have found these visitations most helpful. I have found them invaluable as founder and spiritual father. Quite frankly, I do not know if I could carry this burden alone without some help from an older monastic brother and the bishop. But I often have to humbly submit to input that is different from my own. In a word, it is my opportunity as leader to practice the obedience required of all members. Plus, I am often obedient to the chapter of council when it offers similar opinions that are contrary to mine. No one is above obedience when it is understood properly. A leader can only lead when he or she is really willing to follow and can only teach when he or she is willing to learn.

The last thing is to seek out conferences of other like-minded communities and individuals for *koinonia*, or communion. These occur on international and national levels. It is often difficult to find folks within your diocese who really understand what you are about. Gatherings such as these are well-springs of support and education that strengthen your call. The Congress of New Consecrated Communities in Rome and the Monastic Institute at Saint John's University in College-ville, Minnesota, are great vehicles for this. There are others as well, some of which have come and gone. These always have great presentations. And the personal relationships formed and fostered at such gatherings are beyond price. We put together the Franciscan Eremitical Conference for several years in Graymoor, New York, and also attended a Fellowship of New Religious Communities a few times. These kinds of conferences are always most helpful.

These are just a few more social and ecclesial things that Universal Monks of the New Monasticism often need to be attentive to. We really cannot afford to just tiptoe through the tulips! There is a genuine movement to which we have been called and to which many of us belong. In order for a movement to live and grow, it must take certain steps in order to walk and eventually even run freely within the church and the world. These steps might seem rather mundane and even unspiritual to some. No problem. You might be called to something rather invisible that requires no external expression. But to those called to something visible and invisible in the church and the world, these steps will prove most helpful. But remember, they are no substitute for actually living the life. The external steps without a living, beating heart amount to nothing. But for those with that living heart, these steps help to share it with others and allow it to grow into something far bigger than our own isolated experience. Take the steps. Share the life of the Universal Monk with others. Help a whole new movement to grow!

Appendix 2

The Home Church Movement and the Universal Monasticism

There is a growing movement among Christians today called the Home Church Movement. Today nearly 10 percent of non-Catholics are opting for home churches, and the number is growing fast. These are folks who have given up on the big business, high entertainment, or heavily liturgisized and sacramentalized versions of Christianity. Instead of a professional and often elitist clergy, they rotate facilitators and recognize the special charismatic gifts of members. They celebrate the Lord's Supper in homes around tables. They help members in need by donations to their businesses, families, or home. It's a grassroots thing, not top-down or institutional.

There are similarities and differences between the Home Church Movement and the New Monasticism. Of course, one can be a Universal Monk and a member of the Home Church Movement because one can be a Universal Monk in any religious setting. But historically monasticism has existed alongside and within the greater church.

The similarities are obvious. Early monasticism was primarily a lay movement of folks who wanted to return to a more simple and pure gospel life. They did this in the church in communities or colonies similar to cell groups or quasi-church groups. They were a community within a community. They had their own unique prayer services and leadership. They lived, worshiped, and worked together. They usually began quite small and informal and developed into something larger. At some point they even had their own presbyters to administer the sacraments to their membership. All of this is quite similar to the Home Church Movement.

For the first monastics, strict separation was just a matter of geography. They went into the desert for greater solitude. In the desert there were no existing churches. Villages with parish churches were some distance away. So the first monastics were more separate from the church simply because there was no expression of local church where they now lived. As clergy became monks, sacraments were celebrated at the monastic compounds. As monasticism spread and developed within society and the church, some also went to the local church for Mass on Sundays, but having to leave the monastery for Mass was often seen as an intrusion into the rhythm of their monastic life so was quickly abandoned in favor of Mass in the monastery itself.

There are also important differences. Monastics always saw themselves as members of the church catholic or universal. They never saw themselves as a new church. They submitted to the guidance of local bishops and clergy unless that guidance was at variance of the essence of monastic life itself. Monasteries were often involved in theological issues and usually tried to land on the side of orthodoxy. Only when monks were largely uneducated or when the dispute became so complex that it was almost impossible for the average monk to discern was orthodoxy not maintained. One can think of St. Antony the Great going into Alexandria to help fight the

battles of orthodoxy and persecution at one point in his otherwise solitary life and his lifelong friendship with Bishop Athanasius as an example and model of this relationship.

As monasticism developed, bishops began to see the monks
as great resources for clergy personnel. At first this was resisted. One has only to remember the monastic teaching to "flee
women and ordination" as sources of pride and complication of
life. But later the monks hesitantly began to accept ordination.
At first it was sacramental ministry within their own communities under the direction of abbots who were often laity. This was
still a pretty self-enclosed phenomenon. But later it was for the
purpose of filling the much-needed role of bishops outside of
the monastery. Still later they actually began to accept ordination as priests for parish ministry as well. In our own country we
saw monastics filling clerical and lay ministerial roles in order
to minister to the pioneers arriving in droves to the so-called
New World. This was all a great blessing to the church. At that
point the monasteries became a major part of the institutional
church and even symbols of it, though they always tried to
maintain a higher standard of gospel living.

This is not an entirely bad thing, but it also came at the
price of losing some of its original grassroots purity, freedom,
and we shall even say "charm." At the very least it seriously
expanded the application of the more contemplative charism.
So historically there were periodic monastic reforms that attempted to rediscover that purity. Each reform had the challenge of applying early gospel and monastic values to the
situation in which they found themselves in society. They
withdrew from society in order to renew it spiritually. But
this usually only lasted a generation or two. They started in
obscurity and purity, attracted many followers and admirers,
met with success in the church, and were granted rights and
privileges that turned them into the very thing they were trying to reform. So another reform was needed. They restarted

the cycle and were themselves in need of reform after a couple of hundred years or so. This cycle continues to this day.

Is this a bad thing? I don't think so. It is a source of perennial spiritual renewal in the church and the world. If the monks only separated from the church and the world, they would have no effect on it and would be viewed as a mere socio-spiritual anomaly by most. As it is, monasticism has been a powerful leaven in the dough of the church and the world. Despite many criticisms, it accomplishes powerful things in the world by first withdrawing from it. Part of this is mystical and totally unseen. Some of it is quite pastoral and practical. Monasteries have been powerhouses for spiritual renewal and pastoral ministry all through Christian history. In the words of Evagrius, monasteries and monastics are "separated from all, and united with all" and are peopled by those who have "renounced all, to gain everything."

There is a uniquely modern Protestant complexion to this question of home churches that cannot be ignored. Most all of these modern house churches are non–Catholic/Orthodox/ Anglican in their composition. Their history accepts the notion that if one finds a particular church unacceptable, you can simply find another. When one cannot be found, you are free to found one. This is unthinkable to Catholics, Orthodox, Anglicans, or other high churches nowadays. The splintering of the churches after the Reformation is seen as a problem, not a solution.

For some non-Catholics this is seen as an ideal to be emulated as an expression of the diversity of the invisible church universal. For them, it is exactly how the church is supposed to exist. Catholics also believe in the mystery of the church invisible, but to found autonomous church after church is still simply a break in the unity of the visible church universal.

We do find something similar in high churches, but under a different quasi-church structure based on monastic origins.

For instance, in Catholic circles it is acceptable to start a community or movement but not a separate church. For us, we tend to start what used to be called "orders," not independent churches. In the Catholic Church the House Church Movement would most likely be a movement that met once a week and then went to the local church for Mass on Sunday. At most it would have its own bishop as an apostolic prelature within the larger church, or a chaplain who administered the sacraments to them while retaining nonclerical leadership and structure. I remember my spiritual father telling me that Protestants have churches and Catholics have religious orders and movements. While this is a bit of an oversimplification, he was largely right.

The mendicant movement of the Franciscans, Dominicans, and Carmelites (just to name a few) of the thirteenth century is also a helpful model here. There were many breaking away from the Catholic Church in those days. The Waldensians and the Cathari are the two greatest examples that enjoyed popularity among the people at that time. There were often many seemingly good and even profoundly convincing reasons to break away and found such groups. The church was in real need of renewal and reform. But Francis, Dominic, and the others opted not to break away, tempting as that may have been. Instead, they started communities within the church itself to renew it from within. Though not always understood by the very church they were trying to serve, they remained humbly obedient, even in time of trial and persecution. And it worked. Ultimately this decision to remain united with the Catholic Church was a big reason for their overwhelming success. Other splinter groups drifted off more of less into obscurity, yet predating the positive and negative aspects of the Protestant Reformation.

Today there are non-Catholic Franciscans and monastics to be sure, but they come at the question of church unity from the perspective of an already broken Communion. They are rarely, if ever, advocates of setting up their own church but always seek to be part of a larger institutional expression of the church catholic. (Those who intentionally use such charisms as reasons to form their own church proper are usually not accepted by the larger body of the same monastic or religious charism.) They would not really fall into the House Church Movement, though many in that movement would find some inspiration from them.

So we find many in house churches who are feeling attracted to early monastic spirituality. This is part of the calling to be a Universal Monk. This calling really knows no ecclesial boundaries. But this cannot be accepted without qualification. Authentic monasticism remains organically united with the church universal. It is separated from it relative to its particular charism. But that charism is always seen as part of the church, not separate from it. Furthermore, monasteries never saw themselves as a replacement of the church itself. For us, the New Monasticism is always seen as an alternative society within and alongside modern society. As we say in the BSC Constitution:

> 9. While recognizing the goodness of all creation and humankind, the lifestyle of the community is intentionally countercultural. We are an alternative society living within and alongside modern society. We are also an expression of renewal and reform within the church.

The Universal Monk is "separated from all, yet united with all." That would include the church.